Rustic Fables

Rustic Fables

Charles Miller

iUniverse, Inc.
New York   Bloomington

Rustic Fables

iUniverse books may be ordered through booksellers or by contacting:

iUniverse
1663 Liberty Drive
Bloomington, IN 47403
www.iuniverse.com
1-800-Authors (1-800-288-4677)

ISBN: 978-1-4401-0766-5 (pbk)

Printed in the United States of America

iUniverse rev. date: 12/2/08

The woodpecker's Lament

"I'M ALL OUT OF tree," lamented the woodpecker. To which another voice replied, "Pick another tree." This advice happened to come from the sharp little mouth of a tree squirrel.

"Why?" asked the woodpecker

"Because, stupid, you can go on saving up."

"You're no example. You eat your swag right away."

"While you forget your storage holes," said the squirrel with heat. "Just look at you – and that tree. All your efforts to save your cuisine by hiding it are worthless. You hoard food."

"I'm thrifty."

"Sawdust! You're afraid acorns and trees are going out of style."

"You, I see, are too greedy and voracious. Just look at the little pinecone chewings you leave behind on the ground."

"At least I don't plan to go hungry. I plan to eat."

"Can I help it if there are no more places in this tree for me to bore?"

"Try another dead tree – like that big snag over there, simpleton, and live it up."

With that retort the squirrel ran up the same tree where the woodpecker sat hooked into the bark.He wedged an acorn from its hole and dropped it disdainfully to the ground below. "Poison – these acorns!" he said and chattered He climbed higher, up to an immense limb and deadly in his aim he pummeled the woodpecker with loose acorns shrunk in their holes and with bark that was ready to fall.

The rednecked bird flew away in silence to find another drillable tree in which to store his food.The squirrel searched diligently for another unopened pine cone in which the nut seeds were sweetest. He figured

1

that their quarrel had been over simple matters of life style. After all the forest was big enough for the both of them.

Moral: Every creature has his natural way of going about things. It is not wise to interfere in those laws.

ṪḢE CROCOḊILE
– AND –
FRENCḢY'S ḊOG

"WHO GAVE YOU THE whole possession of this here bayou?" Frnechy's hound dog named Nippy queried the crocodile. The crocadile said in his best English, "My domain is mine -all of it. I keeps out competishun from dogs like yerself."

"Fish and frogs are not my game," said Nippy, the old hound. "I hunts rabbits."

"There ain't no rabbits in here. And even if there was you cain't run on water. Betcha you cain't."

"Betcha I can," said the hound dog. "You ain't never seen me when I run real fast on the water. My master he knows, I reckon."

"Aint you sumpin though – runnin on water! Tell you what, big mouth – "

"Speaking of which," said the dog.

"If you'll just jump in the water here, we'll soon see who can swim over there – to that mense cypress fastest.Abd if you can manage to run, I'll catch rabbits for you."

"Fair nuff. I ain't seen no crocadile yet could whip a good bayou Frenchman's hound dog. No siree."

"Delicious. Let's go then," said the crocodile. The two of them began to swim out across the bayou toward the big bypress roots that stuck up out of the dark water.

"See there. You thunk you'd be crocodile bait but I'm right here longside a you."

Puff, puff – the bayou hound dog swam all the harder as the crocadile merely swished his tail and glided along like a stick on a rising tide. For a ways they were doing fine, the crocadile pretending not to bear Nippy when Frenchy caught sight of the two of them from his bateau. He was about to row out to check his crocadile lures on the cypress limbs when he spotted the pair. He stopped what he was doing in amazement. For believe it to be a fact, he saw that old croc pushing his dog along by the rear, the croc's big, long jaw raised as if to snatch Frenchy's dog into his belly with one chomp He though Nippy was under attack and was about to be eaten. He raised his gun and – bam! bam! – he let fly two rounds. That old crocadile did a flip flop there in the water and instantly sank out of sight. The hound dog paddled over to the boat in answer to his mater's whistle.

The Frenchman dragged the soaking hound aboard and looked him over carefully. Nobody would believe it afterward but Frenchy claimed he saw the teeth marks of that old croc on the dog's back, like he wanted to eat the little critter but did not dare. Yet a dog who could run on water commanded some respect, if even from old crocodiles. If the monster did have tender feelings, it was the kind of tenderness Frenchy like for his stew pot.He tossed a piece of crocadile meat in front of Nippy that night. "C'est bon – better than rabbit, eh?"

Moral: It can be a foolish courage to attempt the impossible.

The Gopher
- and -
The Ground Hog

A GOPHER WHO WAS all out of sorts with his neighbor consulted a ground hog as to what he should do to mend the relationship. The gopher and the ground hog shared the same field and although there was no tunneling between them they enjoyed an earthy conviviality. The ground hog sat upright and listened with patience and understanding, despite his own calendar and ways of living.

"Do you know that my neighbor plans to tunnel right through your living quarters?" the gopher said to the ground hog, hoping to arouse the latter's interest in community development.

"When?" asked the ground hog. "He'll have to do some hard digging because I'm burrowed into clay."

"Don't underestimate my neighbor," the gopher warned.

"You gophers never get along, do you?"

"You can think what you want to, but when he comes scratching at the walls of your dig you'll remember what I said."

"And just what do you expect me to do about the matter?" asked the ground hog.

"Seal him up. Close him out and he'll never break into you dig," said the gopher with vengeance in his voice.

Being weak-willed and wanting to please other ground hogs and, above everything else, avoid the invasion of his burrow by a mere gopher, the ground hog shoveled dirt in front of and down into the tunnel of the gopher who allegedly threatened his abode. This, however, was a colossal mistake by all the terms of field etiquette. For the gophers in this particular field assembled on a night shortly thereafter. They blew, clawed and shoveled dirt with a mean vengeance never before exhibited by any cadre of vigilante gophere. When finished they had completely barricaded and concealed the entrance to the ground hog's den as an act of retaliation and police prevention. While he was asleep he had become a prisoner in his own burrow.

This was a tragic thing for them to do, but the gophers had temporarily at least eliminated the fierce competition from the ground hog for the berries, nuts and corn the hog was stealing and caching in his dig. He had been conducting these forays and hoarding for months, right under the very noses of the gopher community. They had also rid themselves of a fearsome title-holder of the annual job of appearing as harbinger of spring. The gophers had decided among themselves that this kind of "seeing my shadow" nonsense really did no good for anybody. At least – not for this particular ground hog. Life in the field would go on without him who was buried alive.

Moral: Petty spite can destroy the beauty of a good relationship.

tbe pig
~ ANÒ ~
tbe (Dina birÒ

SAID THE MINA BIRD named Rectitude, speaking to the pig in his sty, "You'll never get anywhere with your manners." She preened her black feathers with her golden beak. She Flapped like the rustle of dry leaves around the fence fail. She uttered these words with a harsh throaty scrape of satisfaction, flaunting her hand some beak and wild beauty before the lowly pig. The pig, whose name was Chester, replied to Rectitude's taunts.

"Your voice – how shrill it is – and abrasive. Screech! Screeeech," said the pig, trying to imitate the bird. "You pretend to speak – a fraud if I ever heard one.While I have only a simple oink, oink – and I am done."

"I can sing – and what's more I can talk to my mistress."

"You got that right," said the pig. "You can talk your silly head off and do."

"Well, my fat friend, if you didn't root in the slops and wallow in the mud you'd put on a better appearance."

"Zat so. And who made you a judge of social manners?"

"I did," said Recititude, the mina bird.

"I don't have your social ambitions – and I'm glad I don't," said Chester.

"Don't feel sorry for yourself. Come with me up to the house, if you dare, and I'll really show you ho to behave. My mistress could come to like you and tie a pink ribbon around your neck as a pet."

"Not likely," said Chester.

When they reached the house Rectitude said to her mistress, "Ma'm" – for she was a very polite bird – "ma'm, I have watched Chester for

7

a long time. I know he has bad manners, but if you'll just give me a chance I know I can make a big improvement in his behavior."

"That pig belongs out back!"

"You are in need of a good watchdog. Why not – "The farmer's wife almost died laughing. When she came back down to earth again, she said, "All right, give it a try. But if that pig soils my carpet, we'll have him for breakfast – on the table."

Rectitude promptly began her reconstruction of Chester the pig. She coached him on how to change his mushy snorting oink, oink to a more acceptable oinky, oinky.The sound had polish to it. That one basic change, the mina bird assured the pig, would without a doubt scare off thieves or a coyote after the ducks in the lower pond.

The voice change, however, did not work out too well. Within a week a farm boy, hearing the exotic oinky, oinky of Chester surmised at once that the pig would make a better pet than a normal wallowing pig, and certainly far better as a watchdog than as consumer of slops. He up and stole Chester, keeping him overnight in his own yard. In the morning he had a change of heart and putting the pig on a leash took him to a stock auction. Chester was dismayed and depressed by the sudden turn of events. He reverted to oink,, oink, oink and chose a mudhole along the way to market to recover his pride. The boy was happy. He sold the pig for pork.

Rectitude had flown by hops and starts to the auction yard gate, where she perched atop a post and declared boldly to whomever would listen, "I am too refined and well-trained as a mina bird to deal any longer with that retrograde pig. Let him become ribs and chope." The uncommonly smart talking blackbird thereupon flew off to the farmhouse leaving Chester to be sold for his less refined parts. So ended the start of a fine friendship.

Moral: Act yourself or you'll land in a peck of trouble.

The Cat
- and -
The Canary

A PLUMP, GOLDEN-YELLOW, ROLLER canary began to trill with the most beautiful song one fine sunny morning, going over the arpeggios, its melodies, its thrilling coda chirps with great forte and abandonment. A tawny cat who slumbered nearby was awakened by the music. He stretched, yawned and approached the bottom of the canary cage.

"You woke me up with your loud singing, dya know that?"

"I gotta practice – keep in shape. After all, my voice is worth a thousand of your cat calls."

"What makes you think you've got the best voice in the world," the cat asked.

"As compared to yours, it's beautiful. All I ever hear from you is a cranky meeeooowww.

"You do that very well."

"What - ?"

"Nothing."

"Oh, I've got much more repertory than you think."

"While in my voice there is strength and great timbre – sound, you know."

"Prove it to me then," the canary said.

"Tonight. At night is the best time for me to sing," the cat announced.

"That's good – but I can sing my best when I'm not cooped up. Do you think I can roll out my song behind these brass bars?"

"I never thought of that."

"No, since you've got your freedom you wouldn't – but do you suppose you could – trip the latch to my cage?"the canary asked in a piteous voice.

"I can try," said the cat, cold and methodical.

"Good! Good! I'm so happy I could sing – even at night."

"Please, madam canary. Daytime will be enough."

"When night comes and the woman covers me with an old sack that's the time to let me out. She won't know a thing providing you're quiet. Then we can indulge in our musical – "

"Fight."

"Flight," the canary corrected the cat.

"Flight," said the cat. "Suits me to a mouse."

When the evening drew near and the woman of the house put the black sack over the canary cage, the cat crept up to the sofa in one leap. He sprang onto the rim of the cage causing it to swing with violence several minutes. Using deft techniques he had employed to spring many a mouse trap for the cheeze he touched the latch with the lightest paw. The door to the canary cage sprang open. Opening it wide the bird flew out.

"You are so stupid," said the canary immediately upon gaining his freedom. "You could have made a splendid meal of by reaching into my cage with one of your long legs and paw. My, Oh, my."

Twitting the cat in this manner, the canary fluttered around the room reveling in his newfound freedom. But the cat, whose natural instinct was to pursue and to pounce upon its quary, waited until the bird grew tired and settled upon the edge of a table.

"You have broken into my sleep often enough with your singing. Now it's my turn to break into your daily routine – and finish you off before your mistress comes in the morning. I enjoy the hunt." In the dark the cat had extraordinary eyesight. He gathered himself for one leap and seized the canary around his neck. He then did what all cats do: he devoured his quary, leaving only a few yellow feathers on the gray carpet.

Moral: Don't be too clever lest you outsmart yourself.

ᴛ𝕳ᴇ ᴛᴜʀᴋᴇʏ
- ᴀɴᴅ -
ᴛ𝕳ᴇ ᴡɪɴᴅᴍɪʟʟ

THERE LIVED ON A farm in comparative comfort a turkey who took it into his head that he wanted to fly "like other birds." He desired to flutter up, catching the wind under his wings, soaring sublimely over the fields of grain and leaving behind his old way of scratch and peck. Being a wise bird, as turkeys go, he knew that grain in the neighboring fields was plentiful, especially when the farm boy scattered the corn. He also realized that the cock of the hens in the yard where he had been used to gleaning was too greedy to let him alone after the harvest. The cock was always making a run at him to drive him away from the most succulent leftovers.

It was these realities that inspired the wish within his breast to fly, so that he could fly away to discover fields of grain by himself. To accomplish this end he undertook a simple flying exercise. He flopped, shivered, agitated and squirmed his wings. He tried again and again until at last the cock took pity on him. In his own way, by demonstration, he counseled the turkey that he needed more air lift under his wings if he hoped to fly.That lift would insure his adept performance. This gentle cock furthermore came up with a brilliant idea: he told the dejected turkey that for air lift he could do no better than to try to use the farm windmill for a quick-starter. If he caught its draft he could be airborne and on his way to everlasting true flight and happiness.

First, however, to prove to himself that he owned a native ability to fly, he walked into the barn and mounted up to the hay loft. He emerged above the barn doors and looked down. He sat at some height, just under the barn gable. The cock was dumfounded; for he did not suspect this natural climbing ability in the turkey. In fact, he had always been just a little jealous of the turkey's strength, his wing span and his determined efforts.

Perched aloft the turkey addressed the cock: "The safest way to try my wings first is by soaring."

"You will most certainly crash, turkey," said the cock.

"Gobble, gobble! I know what I'm doing." And so he cast off only to flutter wildly, pitifully down to the ground where he landed in front of the cock and the startled hens with a resounding, dusty kerbump.

"No great distance but a worthy effort," said the cock and the hens clucked their approval. "I tell you, turkey, that if you will try my idea you will surely make it. Just fling yourself into the air currents created by the windmill and you will soar like the eagle." Truly the turkey was secretly envious of the eagle for he had observed it effortless gliding flight many times.

The turkey thus resolved with single-mindedness to try the cock's suggestion. Unfortunately, given to panic as he was, he did not stop to ponder which way the wind blew through the spinning blades. Flappetyflapping up with joy he flew the wrong way, the consequence of his lack of foresight. Instead of being air-lifted by the fanning wind of the whirring mill he was demolished by the rotating blades that drew him in. In an instant he was converted into another kind of bird having torn wings, a leg, many feathers and a piteous final gobble. His feat splintered several of the windmill blades and brought out the farmer shouting wildly and on the run. "Damn dumb bird!" he cried. The cock and his hens thenceforth claimed the borders of he corn field for themselves, without competition from the oppressive presence of the departed turkey.

Moral: No advice at all is sometimes better than bad advice.

ThE fly
– ANd –
ThE SpidER

A SHINY BLACK SPIDER was spinning his web one day when a green bottle fly buzzed in close and settled down to chat. "You know nothing about angles and designs and directions," The spider said, opening up the conversation on a rather spiteful note. The fly was busy minding the spider's business, as flies are intended to do. He watched with a critical eye.

"At least I am not stuck in a smelly old corner with nothing to do but wait for a victim."

"I know. I've heard it all. You are a diligent hunter of food. Yet you are too vagrant to learn anything. To you the world is just one huge garbage pit."

"I don't know about that," said the fly, his pride piqued. "Learn what?"

"Why, web weaving from me. Basic physics and architectural design, old fellow. I could involve you totally," said the spider, mellowing out in contemplation of luring the spider into his web. The fly was, however, a proud fly and felt the sting of the spider's challenge. "I could learn."

"Very well. You see that ring in the center of my web?"

"A wasted effort," the fly said.

"If one strand breaks away from that ring the web stays in place."

"So what do you want me to do – walk out and take a closer look?"

"Not at all. Just understand my engineering. Unlike you I don't do things for nothing. You fly around and what do you accomplish?"

"You're very clever," said the fly. "But what if a bat should fly into your web? Me? I'm too fast for a bat. But you – " The fly began to hummmmzzz with laughter.

"I do not catch bats."

"Nor do you catch flies." Saying this the fly flew up from the spider's corner. He hovered to inspect the product of the spider's pride. No sooner had he done so than a cave bat, hearing the fly's busy wings and all the commotion, homed in on the green bottle pest and devoured him. He thus deprived the patient spider of his meal, while settling the dispute once and for all.

Moral: It is dangerous to meddle in the business of others.

ThE SNAKE
~ AND ~
ThE SCORPION

A POISONOUS SNAKE AMID the chaparral in the high desert said to a scorpion, visiting nearby. "Sir, your poisonous dagger makes my life miserable. I have visions of you every where I go."

The scorpion answered this insult. "Whilest your presence disturbs my peace of mind."

Then let us see who can burrow through that clump of throny sage," the snake challenged. "He who remains shall be accursed. He who passes through shall roam the desert waste land.

"Fair enough," said the scorpion. "I'll let you go first."

Encouraged by the bravado of the scorpion the snake burrowed into the thickest part of the bush. He made it through the entanglement with very little effort. When it came time for the scorpion to assault the bush, he eyed the chaparral with some doubt before starting. Once on the way he clawed his way into the thicket, following the path that the snake had taken. But to his dismay he could not navigate the pricks and snags of the sharp thorns. It seemed as though every time he lifted a claw it caught on a part of the thornbush, either the thorns on the filigree twigs or the needled on the spiked leaves.

The snake looked behind him to see how his competitor was getting along; he saw the scorpion's problem at once. Sidewinders have this kind of sidelong vision. He murmured, "You are too clever. At least I know where I belong."

"Just remember – I've got my troubles getting out of this bush but if I am left behind the desert is mine to rule."

"And mine to roam – a far better life than your silly wanderings, O scorpion.You will be accursed."

"Nonetheless I shall rule this wasteland," the scorpion said in a panic at his plight and not wishing to show the snake the trouble he was in.

"You will rule the hot sun, that's all. You will bake in the desert heat. You will become a stinging flower in the shimmering sands. Men and beasts alike will give you wide room when they pass."

Under the torrid sun the scorpion heard the laughter of the snake in the distance, who ever after, in his enmity toward the scorpion, gave rise to the fable. For this reason the desert thorn is called the scorpion bush. In a way the scorpion still rules the wind-blown sands.

Moral: Enmity will blind one to his reasonable limitations.

The flying squirrel
- and -
The tree squirrel

THERE LIVED AN AN ancient forest a young, ambitious squirrel who, although able to scamper up and down the bark of trees, had an obsessive desire to fly like his neighbor. The neighbor roughtly resembled his visionary cousin, except for a pair of fine wings which he wore whenever he decided to jump across large spaces between trees. Indeed the ambitious squirrel had even watched with envy as his neighbor lept from rock to rock on the mountainside above the forest. He decided to ask the more fortunate flying squirrel how he came to possess such glorious wings.

"How did you go about obtaining those wings?" the ground squirrel enquired with admiration in his small voice.

"Simple," said the bat squirrel, for so he was called among the firest inhabitants. "You just hang by your paws long enough from a tree branch, and eventually your arms will get longer and grow into wings."

"Do you think I might try?"

"I don't see why not," said the flying squirrel, aware of his neighbor's covetous envy.

Without delay, the very next day the ground squirrel began his daily workout routine. He hanged for hours and hoping that his forelegs and his back showed signs of becoming wings, he would extend his jump. At times he jumped so far that he barely caught the branch with his paws. Once he fell to the forest floor, dazed but unharmed. The objective, to grow a pair of fine flying wings, was worth the pain of trying. Then as he extended his jumps from branch to branch he would paddle his feet as if they were wings.

He did fairly well and for a while was happy. Yet he complained to the bat squirrel that he wasn't showing development fast enough

"Then why don't you hang out there in the sunlight? The sun is sure to speed the growth of your wings."

"But is there not some kind of food I should eat that would make my wings grow faster?"

"You might try to chew a piece of ripe fruit, like an orange left by a hiker along the trail."

The tree squirrel tried this new suggestion. But like his stretching exercise he saw very little wing development. At last, despairing of ever sprouting a set of wings, he asked his flying squirrel cousin if there wasn't a shortcut to the final goal. Sure enough there was!

The bat squirrel told his groundling brother that if he didn't mind night life, he could jump from the corner of Mr. Maynard's barn into the chestnut tree that stood in the yard. If he should happen to miss there was some old straw on the ground below that would break his fall. The night air would be so bracing and envigorating that it couldn't help but carry him over the intervening space.

Since the ground squirrel possessed an envy that knew no limits – indeed, he was jealous of the bat squirrel – he would try this latest experiment. He scampered up to the roof of the old barn. He readied himself on the ridge pole and prepared to make the leap. If he failed nobody would see him. One pair of eyes, however, had been watching him, claws set and ready. When the anxious ground squirrel, believing he might start to fly, placed his hind legs in position to jump, his big effort, a barn owl, with the brush of its wings against the night air and the silence of death, swept down upon him and seized him in its talons and bore him away to his nest, flying, alas! , but under the power of the enemy's wings. His envy had led him to ve consumed.

Moral: Envy of another's gift can lead to disaster.

The Cricket
– and –
The Firefly

"You are too noisy," said the firefly to the cricket on a summer eve. "You're always chirping. Looks to me like you'd wear out your legs."

The cricket replied in a caustic tone of voice, "I take it you don't like my love song."

"Bosh!" the firefly exclaimed. "I glow cool when I'm in love but I'm no less passionate.

Just then a cool breeze rattled the leaves in the magnolia tree and the cricket taunted, "Now where are you? A little cool air puts out your light, eh?" Another gust of warm night air shook the leaves and the cricket fell to the ground, into some dead leathery leaves where his night song abruptly ended.

"Changed your tune now, I'd guess," the firefly chided.

The firefly flickered on again and again, gathering his friends around him. For the present the voice of the cricket was stilled. He could only look skyward into the night and wonder at the wasted energy and pointless exercise of a mere fly!

Moral: Bragging rarely improves one's circumstances.

The Thief of The Big Cheeze

IN THE MOUNTAIN VILLAGE of Keswick there lived in the old house of miser Mr. Watson a wee mouse, without pedigree or patron. His one claim to fame – or so he thought – was that he knew better than his fellow mice about cheese traps. Yet as peers they were so generous and so attractive, being boon companions, that he fell in with them. It gave the wee mouse great pride to run with the best band of cheese thieves in the entire household of Mr. Watson. They had stolen from traps which he set regularly, and not once had any of the gang been apprehended by the copper wire spring bale. They had become so skillful at stealing cheese without triggering the snap-trap that in despair Mr. Watson had set out traps everywhere, even loading them with pieces of crusty old bread or leaving them unbaited for the unwary mouse.

Oh, there had occurred some close calls, to be sure, but no deaths yet from mouse traps. The gang had a clean record of successful jobs. Then, as is so often the case, the wee mouse grew more courageous and independent and wanted to start his own theft activity. He thus split off from the old cheese gang and began to rob traps on his own. Be confident that though obscure he was competent. His gang of eight had taught him many things about successful cheese robbery.

On a warm evening, while eyeing an especially big chunk of cheddar in a trap, a lethargic spider idling nearby saw him and said, "Better look out there, buster. You think you're so smart. That there trap has a huge spring in it that'll take off your head. Zip – just like that."

"Stuff!" said the solo thief with arrogance. "I got all mouse traps solved. This one's not for real. Old man Watson is too stingy to put such a large chunk of delicious cheese in one trap." The wee mouse squeeled with laughter.

"Don't you believe it," said the spider. "He's mad he hasn't caught any of you mouse fellows lately. That's the dirt around here. And he's gone overboard to bait this one so's it'll look like a generous offer. Better be careful, mouse."

"I can nibble. I know how to fling my tail so as to spring the trap with a flicker."

"Don't say I didn't warn you," said the spider.

As the wee mouse approached closer, he stopped and examined the chunk of cheese. Another denizen of the household, a small gray lizard, observed the wee mouse pause to comtemplate the huge piece of cheese. "That cheese may be pizoned. Don't put it past the old man," said the lizard.

"Poison! What's that to me? Why I ate some crackers the other night that were laced with acid so powerful it'd peel the paint right off the privy door. But they were good, so good they agreed with me – give me a little indigestion, that's all."

Heedless of the two warnings and coveting the prize, the wee mouse clawed in closer, then flung his fat tail at the cheese. So violent had he acted that his tail ping!" sprang not the trap with the big cheese but the trap nearby with no cheese in it. The wee mouse in his hunger and passion for the one bait had ignored the danger that surrounded him. The bale of the empty trap sprang upward with such force that it caught him right across the neck. From a distance the spider pronounced him dead. And the lizard skirted the place of demise for the next month until the wee mouse had turned to dust and bones.

Moral: Your appetites can be the death of you.

The Headstrong Duck

EVERYWHERE HIS CLAN FLEW, Harvey the duck had to fly in formation with them. He resented this as an imposition on his personal liberty. To show his disdain he flew behind the wedge formation of the flock, catching their turbulence as he flapped along to cool his heated temper. He could hardly wait until the old cripplefoot leader should find a pond and settle down on its surface. He did not have long to wait. The clan slowed and circled as a wedge. Fluttering in total accord they skimmed, legs extended, to a splashy set down. They rocked idly as they hunted for grains and seeds among the pond grasses and tassle debris that blew in from a nearby cornfield. Old Mr. Heller's pond was a succulent landing site – for all but Harvey. He had broken formation with them when they landed and was continuing in flight.

"Where's he going?" a formation duck asked.

"Search me," said the wise leader. "He's a case. He's a real special fowl, he is."

"He's unhappy," said another.

"He thinks we don't know what we're doing," said the wise leader. They were following one of nature's commands for survival on the road.

Harvey continued to fly, winging his way across the spectacular countryside with great abandon and thinking little about where he was headed. It eventually occurred to him that he should land and take a rest. He searched below but he saw no water that was quite so inviting as the water back there, where the others sat feeding this very moment. He also realized with a cold fear that chilled his very wing tips and webbed feet that he was lost. He didn't have the instinct their wise leader had because he had never really led his fellow ducks.

It occurred to him that maybe he ought to turn back and rejoin them. He hesitated to chose between the delicious pond left behind – in it there was safety – and the ground below where he saw a creek winding its way through the rocks and hills. Wisely, he turned back,happy in the thought that this time he had made the right decision. It was ever so beautiful below, but he had better take cover and find security in numbers, for night was falling fast.

Harvey was winging it along, about an hour on his return leg, enjoying the freedom of the experience of independence when he heard a gun shoot off. He heard things zing through the air, right by his ear. He suddenly felt a little sting penetrate his breast, below his dark collar. He thought that maybe he ought to land – but this was not the pond. This was not even the creek he had seen from the air. This terrain was grassland. One of his wings did not work right; it dropped and would not raise itself. Then it stopped working completely, and he plummeted to the ground. This was strange country. He saw none of his fellow ducks around, and those that he recognized were made of wood. He had landed in a cattle pond. Soon thereafter Harvey lost consciousness. Not long afterward he became like one of his wooden bretheren – lifeless. His anarchy of taking the flight law into his own webbed feet had cost him both his freedom and his life.

Moral: The penalty for ignoring competent leadership can be costly.

The ANT
– AND –
The GRASSHOPPER

A FAT, GREEN GRASSHOPPER sat on a fig leaf and scowled down at the ant far below him. "I see you're stuck with making a choice of food you crawl to."

"Food! That's all you think about. At least I do some tunneling and building at times. And what's more, I know my way home. You're lucky if you can swarm your way home."

Stung to the quick, the grasshopper replied, "If I eat this fig leaf completely I do not lose my way."

"Why don't you try it then and we'll see. Me? All I got to do is to follow the ant trail. I'm a roadbuilder, I am."

Disarmed by the ant's frank words and miffed by the ant's contentious spirit, all coming from a thing so much smaller than he, the grasshopper began to eat the leaf boldly and with chewing hunger. He was ravenous. In fact, given the time, while the ant scouted for food, the grasshopper ate the green leaf that supported him and he fell to the ground, into a pool of standing water.

The ant stopped to taunt him. "See there. Your home is in your belly. Mine is in my good sense, my skill in building trails – and in that hill over there. I look where I go."

"Yes, and you got ten million others to help you."

"Speaking of which. Your kind has brought on many a famine in the world. Us? We share and share alike."

"You'll work yourself to death."

"I do not gorge my food," the ant replied. "Goodbye to you, grasshopper. The ant crawled away, along the twig to the branch, from

24

the branch to the limb and down the tree trunk, leaving the grasshopper to flounder in the pool of water with a full belly. When the sun came up to evaporate the water, the grasshopper had drowned.

Moral: Gluttony can kill you.

The Parrot Thief
– and –
The Naïve Hamster

"YOU SILLY FELLOW. You run around in that wheel and that gets you no place."

"Speak for yourself, fancy feathers. Just look at you – perched up on that pedestal and moving your lazy head once an hour to see if you've got a grape coming."

The parrot and the hamster couldn't get together in spirit – they glared at each other, and especially at traces of food stuffed into the trough for the hamster. For his part the parrot ate his tidbits so fast he could stare only at his memories of food.

"You are a good healthy specimen though, hamster. Let's see just how many times you can spin that wheel."

"A thousand at one time," the hamster bragged.

"Come on, fat rodent," chided the parrot. "If you spin that silly thing ten times each and every try, I must be blind. I have fine, glassy black eyes for seeing things sharp and clear. And my colorful feathers are a part of my beauty. On the other claw, I do admire qualities in creatures like yourself who care not so much for beauty in appearance as beauty of spirit."

"I hear you, I hear you," said the hamster, mollified. "Even my mistress speaks of my independent fighting spirit."

"Well said. I wish I had half your spirit," replied the parrot. "Why, I have no doubt that you cans spin that crazy wheel a thousand times a thousand times and scarcely blink an eye."

"Well now, pal, that's kind of you. You'll allow me at least a blink or two. I wouldn't want to see you do too much moulting either, parrot. External beauty is, after all, very important in this life."

"Ah, just so. Are we not becoming fast friends?" The parrot shook out his feathers, scattering several down on to the floor. A blue feather worked loose and flaoted floorward.

"At least you don't have to put up with losing feathers as I do," the parrot said," the parrot said in mock self-pity. "But you do have to endure your smelly wood chips and straw – and the melon they stuff into your face."

"My passion is in fact melon – or pineapple," said the hamster, "with all the tenderness of my mistress."

The parrot almost gagged at this sentiment of the hamster. Yet he had no sooner finished saying these words than his mistress coed to him and stuck a large piece of pineapple through the mesh of the cage.

"You see there. I was right," said the parrot. "Don't forget, little one, you've got to spin the wheel for that delicious tidbit."

"You know, you certainly are a most appreciative neighboy," said the hamster as he climbed into his wheel and began his tireless whirring. The hamster being thus busied, the parrot fluttered down from his perch and seized the pineapple, taking it back to his height where, securing it under one claw he relished the stolen fruit. He squawked his approval of the hamster's exercise and ate on until he had consumed the entire slice. Seeing that he had succumbed to the polished deceit of fancy feathers the hamster could only blink over his disappointment.

Moral: Easy come, easy go for some of life's little rewards.

The Lizard
— and —
The Rock Spirit

A GRANITE ROCK WITH a generous crack in it solicited for tenants after
a light rain in the mountains.

"Ol' rock, what do I care about you," said a ring-necked puff lizard
as he passed by and saw the sign written in moss alongside the crack.

"You'll come around, you'll come around," the rock replied in a
mysterious, weird voice of the wild.

"Never. You offer no comfort to me, O rock," said the lizard.

"I can give you the comfort of security and safety. I am like a fort.
I can protect you if you will let me."

"Nonsense!" exclaimed the lizard and scampered on his way. As he
said this a group of hikers was heading down the trail.

"Look there, wouldja!" their leader shouted. "A ring-necked puff
lizard. Very rare. Get your sack ready, guys," said their leader as they
crept up closer to the lizard. But his small eyes beheld them in all their
monstrous capacity to kill, and he fled toward the rock.

"How about it – take me in?"

"If you wish, said the rock spirit, "but now that you have spurned
me once you will have to pay a penalty."

"What is the penalty I pay?" the puff lizard asked.

"Come in, come in, and you will find out," said the rock spirit. At
that exact moment the giants threw a sack at him – but as it floated
through the air, the lizard scooped up his courage and fled into the
crack in the rock.

"Safe," he said.

"Not altogether," said the rock spirit, for at that moment one of the hikers, his giant face peering down into the rock, exclaimed, "There is out little beasty. Wait! I'll pull him out."

Grasping his tail in two giant fingers, the enemy pulled. With a slight twinge of pain but more as a suprise, his tail parted from his body. He had puffed himself up so tight that the enemy could not budge him from the crack without pulling off his tail.

"You see there. You have saved your life but you have lost your tail. That is the sacrifice I told you about."

"I don't worry. I shall grow another. Then I'll not speak harshly to you again," said the lizard. Deflating himself he listened carefully to the departing footsteps of the enemy. He withdrew from the crack in the rock with a sigh of relief. He and the rock spirit became friends ever after.

Moral: Never scorn the gift offered without strings. It could save your life.

Tbe crocaΔile
– anΔ –
Tbe catfisb

OL' CROC ONE DAY realized that he was getting up in years, old in his skin and slow to launch from the mud into the bayou water. He had lost his bark, which was his warning to other crocadiles of the presence of danger. He carried on his horny back the scars of many territorial fights. He had lost some of his teeth and lately had felt the need to gum his food when he ate. He was very unhappy. Visitors to the bayou in earlier days had wondered why Ol' Croc had not become somebody's watchdog, a pal and hunting guide to a French fisherman. He had possessed the bark of a canine. With a sense of the comedy inherent in Ol' Croc's animated leather, they had watched him grow old, first this year and then the next.

Occupying the same bayou was an uppety catfish named Whiskers who loved to taunt the old monster about the loss of his bark and his missing teeth. Those taunts made Ol' Croc furious. He would thrash his tail when the catfish challenged him to a marathon race. Until lately Ol' Croc had refused such silly proposals outright. But on this particilar day, when Whiskers chose to malign the crocadile's agility in the water, Ol' Croc had had enough. He accepted the swimming duel dared by Whiskers.

"You swim from this here bayou de Orleans to the Bayou La Croix. That's five miles," the crocadile said. "You swim that far, you little piker, and I'll hunt for you personally the rest of my days. And I mean – to eat you."

"You're on," said the catfish, using crocadile-trap lingo. And so they began.

Whiskers, of course, swam over and under and around Ol' Croc, taunting the reptile the whole way. For the catfish, though appearing sluggish, can swim with might when he wants to.

Ol' Croc just kept on swimming, moving his tail lazily and gliding past the fisherman's shack, where Frenchy's bateau rocked idly in the shade of the cypress. He glided past the oil well and into a main channel, then down-headed toward La Croix bayou.

Meanwhile the catfish was so cocky and sure of himself that he gathered a school of his kind together. Since he knew that he would win the race, he planned to make Ol' Croc feed the entire clan when he swam into the bayou late. Ol' Croc saw them coming and dove down deep into the murky depths of La Croix Bayou. The school swam over his head, while he stubbornly kept down awaiting the right moment to put his own plan into action. He was, after all, a wise old crocadile and not to be outmaneuvered by a mere catfish.

When the school had passed over his head, he swam up behind them. He opened his immense jaws and snatched into his belly several catfish with one bite. The others did not notice this deft rear-guard attack. But Whiskers, knowing a thing or two about the treachery of all crocadiles, cut out of the school, a catfish dropout. At the precise instant when he did this Ol' Croc swallowd the rest of the catfish suckers who, relying on their friend's persuasion had hoped for free handouts by the crocadile for the rest of their lives. For his part, Whiskers was so frightened by this unexpected turn of events that he idled off at a distance, yielding the contest to Ol' Crocl

The primieval beast had come off best in this battle for survival because he hadn't lost his bite after all, although he had lost his bark. As Ol' Croc swam leisurely away he shed tears over the loss of Whiskers' catfish friends, despite the reality that this entire event had been a fish idea. Also, the final annihilation of school friends gave rise to the expression that when one cries meaningless tears they are crocadile tears.

Moral: Never take your competition for granted.

31

A FROG TRADEOFF

A SLIMY GREEN BULL frog croaked all night until his voice was quite hoarse and sore. He sought relief by eating some algae. In the morning he complained to his colony about laryngitis; the frog equivalent is a breathy old-age sound. Also, his mouth was painfully stretched because of his continual puffing up. In the frog world, he was "ready to cast off."

"Simpleton!" a lady frog said to him when she learned of his plight. "Why don't we take turns croaking? The sound will produce a lovely cacaphonic musical rhythm."

"An excellent suggestion," a fat, friendly bull put in. ""Your voice is much too loud as it it."

"Sometimes, darling, we can't hear ourselves croak," the lady frog confided.

"Ribet, ribet – I'm so sorry. I thought I was upholding the reputation of the colony for warm and friendly frog sounds

"We really ought to stick together on this," said another bull frog. "Ribet, ribet, ribet!"

"You have such a jocular way of putting things, " said the ailing frog.

Numbering some seven or eight frogs, the entire colonly joined in in the croaking conspiracy. They no longer feared to be voiceless and deprived of the capacity to call to their mates or to announce the presence of summer warmth and pleasant waters.

To this day humans can hear the alternating rhythm of the frogs in the pond or on the bank of the creek. Word got around fast after that first attack of laryngitis in the throat of a complaining bull frog. Frogs everywhere discovered that the system was imenently workable - as all level-headed bull frogs can tell you. It dispels the sore-throat gloom and brightens up the night with voluptuous, alternating voices of frog delight.

Moral: A friend will willingly share your burdens if you'll only let him.

Tbe CROW
~ ANÒ ~
Tbe wbite Òove

A GLOSSY BLACK CROW had watched a white dove fly by his territory often and knew where he came from. He was envious of the dove who, to his surprise, landed on a tree branch nearby to his limb. He wanted answers. He decided to dialogue with the dove.

"Why do they always make you the emblem of peace and all that other garbage?"

"It is because of my purity," said the dove. "I am the bumbol of everything that is peaceable."

"Rot!" said the crow. "I shall try you."

"Please do," said the dove.

"Then come fly with me for a time and we shall see."

So the dove took off in flight with the crow and they were a pair. Other crows joined them and soon there were many black crows that flew down into a corn field. The white dove was among them.

"Are you lost, little one?" they enquired. The dove knew better. He knew why he was there. In fact he knew what they were up to. He saw that they wanted him to make peace with the scarecrow, indeed, to neutralize and make a pacifist every scarecruw they should ever encounter.

When they had come to their first cornfield,therefore, and had settled down from flight, the first crow said to the dove, "Go make peace with that rag man in the field there. Maybe he will cotton up to you and we can eat in peace."

The dove didn't want to alienate his black friends, for he wanted to preserve his image; yet he knew that the scarecrow had a job to do for the farmer. Wishing, however, to be free of crow coercion, he flew up and landed on the hat brim of the scarecrow. He addressed the rag man. "Why is it that you are hostile all the time?"

"Why? I? Me, hostile? Can't be. I simply stand here and, being dumb and lazy, I don't say a word or put up a fight. But those flakes of burnt stubble – they are guilty of theft – every last one of them. They've got to pass along their guilt somehow. I guess I'm the fall guy."

"If you were asleep you'd be just as guilty, according to them."

"You hit it, pal," said the scarecrow to the dove. "If you'd like to build a nest under my hat you're welcome to do so."

"Oh, no thanks. That won't be necessary, but I appreciate the offer."

"You'll always be safe with me."

"I know. Crows are afraid of their own bad reputation."

"You have hit it again. Say, you are bright! But why are you white?"

"I try to keep the peace."

"Well, it needs keeping around here, let me tell you, Pal. Them crows won't let a rag man rest one minute."

"I would have become avaracious and hostile. Who knows. I might have begun to crow also. And – I'm a dove."

"Just remember my offer – if you ever get stuck, white dove."

As the crows began to fly about and to eye the neighboring fields, the first crow abruptly flew in and landed on the coat arm of the scarecrow.

"Not good for you to be hanging around scarecrows."

"Why not?" the dove asked in simple dismay.

"Scarecrows are not all they appear to be. They are counterfeit men. They have the heart of the farmer who put them there."

"His labor is honest. Yours is not," said the dove.

Reasoning along this line, he took flight and returned to the wire cage where his young master had fed him for so many months. He was contented that he had explored and had discovered the truth about crows,whom he had formerly envied so much for their freedom and carefree spirit. He preferred peace in captivity; after all, he could still fly about the countryside in the daytime. And he had a sanctuary in the hearts of all rag men of the fields, the peace-loving scarecrows.

Moral: In freedom there are responsibilities. Absolute freedom is anarchy.

the two sheep dogs

Dogs do not always get along together. There lived on a farm in upstate California a dog named Spot. He was very disgruntled, always whining, barking incessantly and generally getting in the way around the house. For he had become a house pet, a status that made him next to worthless out in the field. One day he confronted his canine friend, both of whom were in the employ of their master Tvarish. The second dog, and by far the more capable at herding sheep, listened carefully to Spot.

"Our master makes you overwork." This was said out of envy of Shep's favored position as a working dog.

"So he makes me overwork. Let me tell you, Spot, I like my work."

"He doesn't feed you enough. Me? I eat as good as the folks in the house. And I like their food. He throws you only a bone."

"That's good for my teeth," Shep replied.

"Why don't you rebel?" Spot asked. "It's easy. Just bite him or one of the lambs and he'll reward you with freedom from work."

"I know you don't like me to come around here – but why should I bite my master?"

"Why! Why, to express how you feel," said Spot. "After all, that's how I started out, and they finally gave in to me."

"I ought to put down our master – is that what you mean?"

"Rebel, rebel – for the sake of personal growth, "said Spot. "How do you think I got this soft job?"

"I don't honestly know. You tell me. There are laws that prohibit open rebellion by dogs, you know."

"If you'll bite him just a little nip, that'll certainly make him sit up and take notice." Shep responded with a bark. "When you do it wag your tail. He'll understand. You want a promotion, don't you?"

"That's not the way to get it. Besides – to what?"

"Do you want to go around all your years here being ordered about and kicked and abused? That's a dog's life. Take your destiny into your own hands, Shep."

"You really think I could get to come into the house from time to time?"

"I'm sure you could. Trust me," said Spot.

So Shep would do as he was told by his friend. It would be just a little nip. That's surely make the master come around and take notice of his fearless quality.

Before too long an opportunity presented itself.Shep snapped at the hand that fed him a bone one night. As a consequence his master thought hard about about giving him away – or bringing him indoors. But who'd want an ungrateful and possibly dangerous sheep dog around children? Instead, master Tvarish sent Shep to the dog pound. Spot was then put out into the field to control the sheep. His advice had boomeranged on him. To take his place as a pet in the house master Tvarish purchased a lady poodle, one of the most contemptible excuses for a dog that ever came to the farm. Spot said so with conviction.

Moral: Do not tamper with justice or you scheme may go awry.

The cuckoo bird finds his niche in life

A CUCKOO BIRD LIVED in a tree where the other birds sang. They sang in the early morning and late at night. The cuckoo was fascinated by their clear, melodic voices and musical talents. He asked a mocking bird one day about his variety of notes and the mockingbird replied, "You've got to have a good musical ear and a good memory to sing like me."

The cuckoo asked the lark the same question, and the lark said, "My shrill fluting voice is a gift from the woods spirits." The cuckoo was despondent. He had on a silly two-note song. He told his sad tale to another of his kind one day and the other cuckoo's reply was: "You need only two notes, no more. If you're so meloncholy I know where you can be heard often. You will enjoy comfort and security and happiness – and no more of this laying your eggs in some other bird's nest. Go ask Herr Wasach about a singing job."

From there the unhappy cuckoo went to the clock shop his friend had recommended. He applied for a singing job at Herr Wasach's and he was hired at once. He would have to sing out not two or three times a day but seventy-eight times every day and seventy-eight times every night. Everybody would have to listen to him then, and so long as somebody pulled his chain weights he could exercise his singing voice to its fullest.

The cuckoo bird was very happy with his new job. He no longer felt stressed out. And he lived to a ripe old age behind his little door, far away from the musical competition of his peers.

Moral: Envy will limit and eventually destroy talent.

THE COW
— AND —
THE BUFFALO

SHE WAS AN ORDINARY COW. She had simply wandered from the herd when a furious, blinding snow storm sprang up. The wind chill, the freezing air and heavy flakes of snow were already smothering the prairie flatland.

Yet the cow cropped the visible tufts of wild grass with unabated relish.

"Where do you think you're going?" one of the buffalo grazing nearby asked the cow.

"Out to pasture," said the cow with bovine nonchalance.

"Don't you see there's a snow storm on us, maybe even a blizzard," the buffalo said.

"What! You're afraid of every cloud in the sky."

"Look, cow. This is no ordinary cloud."

But the cow went on cropping and chewing until at last she was compelled to take notice and heed the cold weather.

"Better get in under some shelter," the buffalo warned.

"You're no better than I am," said the cow.

"You know, in some ways we are, you slickhaired ignoramus."

Paying some heed to the words of the buffalo, the cow began to amble. But she began ambling in the wrong direction. "I see some of my fellows over there," she said.

"These are our fellow," said the buffalo. The other buffaloes looked up and regarded the cow through their shaggy heads of hair, shaking their huge, bearded faces in disbelief.

"Tell me another," was the cow's retort. "I got eyes. I can see ," she flaunted with unruffled disdain, Heedless of the warning of the buffalo the cow headed away from the distant farm. Gusts of wind laden with snow were sweeping across the plains. The cow slowly turned around, pulling up almost completely covered bunches of grass on the way. The wind raised the stiff hairs in her hide. She walked past the buffaloes that were bunched together at a distance. They followed her sorrowfully through black eyes; she was a good hour away from the farmhouse and barn. The snow began falling more heavily. She did not see her fellows anywhere as she walked. It was not long before her strength began to leave her. She knew that she would be doomed if she stopped. Instinct told her. Yet in a very short while the wind-drifted snow became impenetrable. She floundered, got up, floundered again. Nature was pitiless. She was soon bewildered. When she reached a fence, etched with snow, she knew that she was lost, at the edge of an unrecognizeable field. There is where the farmer in his snowmobile found her.

Moral: Stubbornness in the face of reason is a damning vice.

The Hawk
~ and ~
The Tortoise

A HAWK FLEW DOWN close to a tortoise to see what he was up to. The natural curiosity of the hawk has meant death to its cousins on many occasions. The hawk settled in a thorn tree and said to the tortoise that was making its way over the sandy ground: "You crawl along as though you are pulling a rock twice your size. How do you ever expect to see the countryside as I see it?"

To this insult the tortoise replied, "If I had wings I would fly like you do. But I prefer my perspective. I see things in much finer detail close up."

I see my meal from a great distance. That gives me an advantage," the haws replied.

"I find his tracks and can pursue my quary at a leisurely pace."

"Surprise is my strength," said the hawk.

"When I see tracks I know I'm going to find delectable food. I'm not above trying dead snake meat. After all – "

While they were in the middle of their quarrel a noise crossed the path of the tortoise. "Lazy bum – always in the way!," the horse neighed. "I almost kicked you into eternity."

"You see there," said the hawk, "your fate is to endure insults. While I fly far above them."

"At least I shall live to see another day. The horse will die carrying a man around the countryside. I shall die only when old age takes me."

"May your hardshelled, phlegmatic soul perish in a sheol," the hawk screamed. He then flew away – but the last sound he ever heard came not from the horse or the tortoise. It came from the muzzle of a hunter's gun, patiently leveled at him while he sat in the thorn tree. His words to the tortoise were his last. He fell from the skies the victim of his daring and his pride.

Moral: The enemy rarely announced his presence.

The Monkey
– and –
The Dog

Said the monkey to the dog, "Why do you sleep so much?"

Said the dog to the monkey, "I cannot help it. I was born that way."

Said the monkey, "You are a lazy one. You sleep at night on your master's porch. Then you sleep in the daytime in the outdoor sun."

Growing impatient with this jabbering of the monkey, the dog challenged the anthropoid showoff. "Tell you what, monkey. You run around that tree one time and let me watch you. Then tell me you can run faster than I can because you are always so wide awake."

The monkey answered with a braggart's pride. "You can't put me on, dog. Monkeys leap, jump and scamper all the time."

To these words the dog replied, "Go on witcha! Then jump into that tree. Let's see just how quick and agile you really are."

The monkey accepted the dog's challenge, swinging up amid the branches, but as he landed a cage door slammed shut and trapped him. The dog marked the tree as his boundary, all the time grinning at the smart-alec monkey.

Moral: Be wise. Know your adversary.

THe BEAR
~ AND ~
THe CAMPeR

A PARK CAMPER THOUGHT he would like to feed the bears near his campsite. His wife said "they are so cute." Wishing to acquire a more intimate contact with nature,he scattered granola around on the ground. The aroma came even to his own nostrils. He waited. Soon a large black bear showed up a short distance away. Their dialogue went something like this:

"Why not try my little snack, bear?"

"I wouldn't want you to waste it, Mr. Camper." Actually the bear was more polite that the camper, whose impatience urged him on.

"Then come on. Try it. It's much better than berries and it's a lot of trouble to fish in the river, I know. We both know that."

The bear was wary, yet he was hungry for the sweet granola, so hungry that he began to salivate from the mouth. He approached the hand that held the bag of granola. He sniffed along the ground and raised his nose in the air to further verify the gift he was being offered. The scent was overpowering.

"Here, bear," the camper again entreated and jiggled the bag. As the bear approached the playful camper, the man withdrew the bag to taunt the beast. Now his son wanted to take a picture of nature in the wild; he was itching to get a good shot of the black bear with its pink mouth wide open, reaching for the offering of food.

"Get closer to him, daddy, so I can get both of you in the picture."

Daddy complied. He again held out the bag of tasty granola. But, like the boy and the camper, who did not know where good sense ended and insanity began, the unreasonable bear reached out for the bag of sweet grain, standing on its hind legs to waddle a step or two forward. Suddenly, it dropped to all fours and lunged.And wouldn't you know it! The bear bit off the fingers of daddy to provide a perfect shot for his son. The man screamed in pain, while the slobbering bear nuzzled the bloody bag on the ground and the boy shouted, "Get away from my daddy, you terrible nasty old bear!"

The bear and the man both got more than they bargained for, if you can call their exchange a bargain.

Moral: Kindness to animals in the wild has severe limitations.

the fly who loveò to party

AN ENORMOUS, WELL-DEVELOPED BOTTLEGREEN fly was circling the pastry case one day, looking for a way in. He kept up his buzzing flight, at last landing on the glass. He hoped that the baker would open up the case while he waited patiently to fly in. This happened several times.

"Shoo fly! Cursed pest. I'll get you yet. "The baker took after the big fly with a swatter, but he repeatedly missed. The fly landed atop the case once more. He surveyed the delicious morsels under the glass. He was famished. The bread had wrappers on it, the cookies were in a jar; the ovens in the back room were too hot. No, he decided to stay, and since he was lonely and flew around by himself he thought he would rest and just watch. Soon there buzzed by a small gnat, well known in the fly community and full of pep and love of life.

"Come with me. I'll show you where there's a good time to be had.
"Where?" the greenbottle fly enquired.
"Down there – where all that noise is going on."
"No, that place is occupied by the local pests and other competitors," the fly said.
"So what!" the gnat replied. And he flitted away. But the fly's curiosity was aroused. What he needed was a little more joy in life, like that of the gnat. He like what felt good to him and everything that tasted delicious, especially sweets. Why not? That was his nature, his soul food. He lifted off and flew down to investigate the party scene. There they were. some of them his friends, out cold from the booze served. "Must be a real glut of a party," he thought. "Maybe I ought to go in and get acquainted. Can't hurt me. And looks like drinks are on the house."

Then he noticed a hornet sitting atop the wainscotting, lost.

"Great bash going on in there."

"Not for me," said the hornet. "I got to tell you man, you're a real chump."

"Man, oh, man! What a party! What booze. I deserve it."

The big fly with the green velvet back flew into the party and was instantly greeted with an electris hiss. He then became one of the crowd of the dead.

Moral: Having fun like everybody else can be the death of you.

тbe Ouck
~ anO ~
тbe ᙣilleR

A DUCK WANDERED DOWN to the corn mill one day in hopes of picking up a free meal of corn at the doorway, where from time to time kernels of corn would spill onto the ground from farmers' sacks. Fortune was with him this day, for a farmer, hauling by a rickety wagon and careless of tying the ears to his sacks had spilled some kernels of corn on the ground.

"Sir," said the duck to the mill owner when he stepped outside to check on the weather, "if you'll let me eat the kernels of corn that fall by your mill doorway, I can keep the entrance to your mill looking neat and clean." The miller pondered the offer and then said to the duck, "Only if you promise not to get in the way and – not to quack."
"Agreed," said the duck. They struck a bargain.

By the end of the day, however, the duck had found only a small handfull of kernels to eat and he was still hungry. Every sack that a farmer unloaded tantalized him. The miller came outside to help load a wagon with the finished corn flour. He saw the hungry duck standing to one side and pitied him.

"My wife has promised me that if I sweep the inside of my mill and keep it tidy, she will reward me with a fine meal this Sunday."
"That's just my kind of work," said the duck, "making the corn and grain that is dropped disappear."
"Well, if you think you want to," said the miller with hesitation, "I suppose I can give you a try. My helper boy around here hasn't shown

up for two days and I'm in need of cleaning the inside of my mill."
Again the miller and the duck closed a deal and the duck was happy.

He kept all fragments of meal and especially whole kernels from
collecting under the feet of the busy miller. That made the latter quite
happy, and so he called his wife down from their lodgings above the mill
to see the pleasing results of the duck's labors. But – travesty upon good
luck! – she assumed that the miller had caught and penned the duck,
intending to cook him for their Sunday dinner. She seized a broom and
chased it quacking into a corner. She was all set to demolish the noisy
creature with one blow from a wooden stave when the miller stepped
between them.

"Don't kill that fine duck, Gretchen. He has done me a real service
by keeping the mill floor clean of corn grains and chaff. We will not
have to pay the boy to sweep up if we keep the duck around here."

"You always was a good manager," Gretchen agreed.Overhearing
this arrangement the duck quacked his approval. From then on the
duck lived a life of safety, comfort and luxury within the mill by keeping
the plank floor clean of corn , meal and sweet husks.

Moral: By hard work you can overcome many obstacles.

tbe snail

A GARDEN VARIETY SNAIL spotted a lucious bed of hyacinths down the brick path of the garden. He hungered for them. Their leaves promised an aphrodesiac holiday. Although they grew far away, he would have them even if it took all night for the trip. Girding himself up and checking his lubrication apparatus, he started out.

As he headed down the path a garden spider stepped between two leaves to watch. "Where're you going, you lazy goop?"

"To eat some hyacinth leaves."

"Way down there?"

"I have time. What's it to you. Those distant leaves are my favorite food."

"You don't say. You're much too big for me to digest, but I have feeling for my fellow foragers. And you, O snail, are one of them. We must stick together. My only problem with you is that when you make the leaves silvery with your slime I can neither attach a suitable web or attract my own favorite dinner course. Gnats are in season, you know."

"I'm sorry," said the snail. "I never imagined."

"No, you're too slow witted, and I can see why. You've got that huge spiral shell to drag along. Man, O, man ! If I had to do that I would be grounded also."

"I get used to it."

"I'll bet you do,' said the spider. "But hear me, silly fellow, these marigolds are the best. I mean the best! You can't match them even with your hyacinths."

"They give me indigestion."

"Not these. These are sugar sweetened in the sun. You'll relish them. You'll soon forget all about your hyacinths."

"Don't be too sure about that."

"Before sundown come on over,' said the spider. "At least tomorrow you won't be exhausted with the trip down the path. And I have to tell you, I am pushing marigolds. They are delicious. And – they are a closer trip."

"I suppose I could be persuaded to give them a try."

"Bully! There's the fellow. Come on over," cajoled the spider, swinging nimbly from his web and waiting for the snail to cross into his territory.

"I just might, I just might. They are at least a shortcut – cool, dool, down that edge of the path."

"Now you're thinking the right way, the gardenly-correct way."

The snail made a track directly across the brick path and into the gardener's freshly turned flower bed. The deprivedcreatureloved sugar with his greens and so he gorged himself heavily. That night he succumbed to plant poison. The spider completed his web, smiling with cold disdain on the final death gasps and contractions of the lowly garden snail.

Moral: Don't take shortcusts to gratify an appetite. The outcome could be calamitous.

TWO COOPERATIVE FLIES

A VENTURESOME FLY FELL into a man's bowl of vegetable soup where he sat spooning away in a rather exclusive restaurant. The insect was unseen by him because he was far-sighted. The soup was minestroni; it belonged to a first class table de hote. It contained chunks of potatoes, carrots and meat. The man's eyesight was, in fact, so poor that he failed to observe another fly buzzing in the vicinity and the usual restaurant noises obscured the whine of the insect.

The fly trapped by gravity and liquidity in the bowl of soup was filled with desperation. Try as he might to crawl up the sides of the bowl or to rest on a floating raft of potato , he could not rescue himself. He would fall back into the hot, stirred liquid, flounder, fanning his wings to keep cool. Every time he tried to catch a ride on the man's spoon, the man blew upon the coup to cool it and only blew him back into the bowl. These were nervous moments for one of God's little insect.

Despairing as he was and about to drown, he clung to hope, for another fly, drawn to the soup, zoomed down close to the same bowl. They obviously shared a liking for minestrone.

"This is the best soup but this is the worst predicament," said the drowning fly.

"I see," said the other fly five hundred times, one from each eye lens.

"The man doesn't know I'm here," said the hapless first fly.

"We'll have to use our wits," said the second fly.

"Like what – drop his tie in the soup for me to crawl up on?"

"You know the old garbage about the more noise you make the bigger the attention you get."

"Don't be funny. I'm drowning. I'm desperate."

"It's good the man thinks you're a grain of floating burnt rice."

"Keep your sad jokes to yourself. You see that big piece of potato.?"

" Sure do."

"Well, if you'll land on it he'll see us both and pick us out."

"Great idea! I'll just buzz him in his ear to get his attention."

The rescuer fly then flew down and together they fanned the soup vigorously. They combined their sizzling sound like a veritable dance of death. Focused onto his bowl of minestrone by the combined fanning sound of the two desperate flies,the man shouted his outrage to the waitress. She came hustling up to the table and removed the bowl. She pitched its contents and the two liberated flies into a pail of garbage out in back of the kitchen. There, congratulating each other, they both successfully crawled out of the pail. They dried off and flew away, each going his own way with but the memory of the deathly escape to make them wiser and harder to swat.

Moral: Collaboration in a crisis can often save one's life.

Tbe mouse
~ and ~
Tbe Tom cat

A WEE MOUSE ABOUT to be eaten by a big tom cat in an alley said, "Sir, you have nine lives and I have only one. If you will lend me one of yours I'll surely pay you back."

"How can I do that?" the tom cat asked.

"Very simple, Sir Tom. Just fetch up that trap over there – the terror of my life – and drop it into the sewer. Then I shall be forever grateful to you. Have one, save one, ol' boy. If I get an extra life from you, you can count on me to stick around- your chance at two instead of one mouse. Two for the price of one."

"That's a bargain, little mouse. I didn't think about that."

The cat did as the mouse suggested, while the mouse waited at the bottom of the fire escape for the cat to return. When the tom saw that the mouse was still standing where he had left him, the mouse said to the cat."What you see now is one of the lives you loaned me. Have you forgotten how I tasted in my first life?"

"I never caught you or ate you a first time."

"Ah, Sir Tom, but your appetite deceives you, and if you eat me again this time you will never recover your nineth life."

"Who wants it anyway?" said the cat. Just as he was about to pounce on the wee mouse the little creature scurried away with his one life, never again fearing the dreaded trap. He was a pragmatist and knew he could manipulate the tom cat.

Moral: Make artful use of a synergistic accomplice for a worthy objective, such as survival.

ThE AMBITIOUS BOOKWORM
~ AND ~
ThE LAZY SILVERFISh

SAID THE BOOKWORM TO a silverfish one night,when all the library lights were out: "I have this inexpressible, gnawing hunger for knowledge. So I've decided to eat my way through the enclyclopedia."

"What a stupid fellow you are!" replied the silverfish. You can get the same effect by chewing on the title pages only."

The bookworm who was far more intelligent than the silverfish gave him credit for, said, "If I know a little something about all things, I can fill in the details latter. That way I will sound learned."

"I am much core impressive when I can quote the titles aptly," said the silverfish.

Ignoring the strategy of the silverfish, the bookworm started to bore laterally on the index to the encyclopedia. He was kept very busy for the rest of his life by feeding solely on the events and accomplishments of men. The silverfish scurried about, happy in his role of scavenger of titles. Both insects died before they ever reached their dream of total knowledge through the consumption, by the bookworm of erudite data or by the silverfish of learned titles. The librarian never asked them to recite what they had learned, for the process of mastication is not the same as integration by digestion. Both the bookworm and the silverfish would have failed dismally the latter test. That's why they must be eradicated from all libraries.

Moral: Profound knowledge humbles; superficial knowledge puffs up.

ᴛ**ꞓꞓ** ᴄᴀᴛ
~ ᴀɴꝺ ~
ᴛꞓꞓ ᴍɪʟᴋᴩᴀɪʟ

ONE DAY A CAT was so famished for milk it thought about tipping over a pail of milk that stood on the floor, just inside the barn where three cows had been milked. He licked his chops and mewed and paced about. He grew hungrier by the minute. He at last hit upon a plan. The pail was too heavy for him to overturn. If he could drop stones into the milk it would splash over the side and he could then enjoy a feast by himself. It would be a long and tedious business but he could look forward to the delicious results.

One by one he found the right-size stones for his sharp teeth and small mouth and he dropped each of them carefully into the milk pail. The stone made a strange clank on the bottom; the milk hardly moved at all.

He persisted, again and again, yet with almost the same results. He was about to give up. He kept on dropping stones into pail only stopping from time to time to rest. Abruptly, with the last try, he saw trickle of milk run down the side of the pail, and he was much encouraged. The cat doubled his efforts until the milk began to run copiously down the sides of the pail. As it did so he lapped it up with a famished appetite. Indeed he had discovered that, like producing a spring of milk, all he had to do to succeed in tapping this vast reservoir was to continue to drop stones into the milk.

At last he wearied of the taste of milk and his labor to obtain it. He knew though that he had discovered a way to obtain a fresh supply of milk any time he wanted. And he could lap at the milk spring until dawn; the farmer's son had set the pail there by the door to cool. The cat had a method; that was the important thing. He ought never again to go hungry.

Moral: Necessity often gives rise to invention.

the goose
~ and ~
the watchdog

A BIG, AGGRESSIVE, MEAN-TEMPERED goose wandered into a neighbor's yard one day and the farm watchdog chased it down the road a ways to drive it off.

"Whatsa matter with you, dog? Don't you see I ain't causing no trouble?"

"You're in my territory, goose. The sooner you learn that the better."

"Just who do you think you are, dog?" the goose asked with a beligerant honking – "onk! onk! onk! onk!" flailing its yellow bill like a small club.

"I am the family watchdog," said the dog proudly, giving his adversary a short bark of warning.

"I've come here to take over your job," said the goose, honking beligerently, thrusting its neck at the mongrel farm dog.

"You! Why you make friends with anybody!"

"You don't know who to bite and not to bite," the goose replied.

"You see that man coming down the road towards the house. I ain't never seen him before. Go get rid of him, goose, if you're such a good watch thing."

The goose set out to chase off the stranger but instead the stranger threw some pieces of bread in front of him. They were dainty and delicious looking, and the goose readily disposed of them. He didn't at all like attacking the stranger; instead he waited for more of the same handout. And surely they came. The dog, standing at a distance, saw the goose taunting him with honkings and swings of his long neck. He responded by making a run at the stranger. For this effort of defense the stranger heartily kicked him.

"There, you see. I saw that man meant well, while you thought he meant only harm," the goose scorned the dog.

"You are revolting. You think you can tell one stranger from another by his handouts, do you, goose?"

"I certainly do."

About then a child came down the road and the dog went up to him, wagging his tail. The goose honked excitedly to chase the boy away. "There, you see I was right," said the goose. "You wag your tail and the boy came to steal a chicken. I can tell."

"You are silly," said the watchdog. "You can't tell an innocent child from a wicked invader."

"Oh, yes I can. The invader always pretends to be innocent. The boy did not pretend. But all the same I saw he had wicked intentions."

"Now you are getting above your depth," said the dog.

Just then another stranger, a man with an axe walked into the farmhouse year. The goose, seeing he meant no good honked furiously at him and ran at him with his open beak, intending to bite him. Indeed he got so close to the man that he felt a sack thrown over him and he was swept into it. He realized the string was tied. The last sound the goose heard was the dog barking in laughter.

"I go by smell. You go by your poor eyesight,you silly goose!"

The goose became the man's dinner, since it was his goose that had wandered off. The watchdog returned to the farmhouse, disgusted with the whole wretched scene of the attempted takeover.

Moral: Bragging could land you in an oven one of these days.

The Termite
- and -
The Spider

A LONELY TERMITE WAS feeling sorry for himself in the presence of a large, brown spider one day.

"This old house is about to fall down. Then I shall have no place to go to eat." The truth was that generations of his friends and relatives had feasted on the foundation wood and gnaw ed through many of the rafters, and they were the cause of the house about to collapse.

"Tell you what," said the spider. "I know all the good places to eat. You just follow me." So the termite crawled into line on the two by four and followed the spider to an ancient historic piece of pine, under the eaves, that was untouche dexcept by age.

"Marvelous for the appetite," said the spider. "I eat here often and I always manage to leave my fine signature behind."

"I'm not a gourmet like yourself," said the termite."Almost any old board will do, providing it has the proper nectar sap in the wood."

"Whilest I am a specialist. Unlike you I like live game and always manage to snare a few specimens on the wing."

"Cellulose is very good for the digestive tract, I find," said the termite. "Fortunately for me the owners of this house do not trouble me as I chew my food well and discover new eating timbers. I like seclusion, you know."

"No I didn't. My style is high-profile," said the spider. In this way the termite and the glossy spider shared dark confidences.

Drawing his eight legs straight, the spider said," I see your an insect of discrimination. Let me show you around."

"Just briefly. I have a board that I must start on. It should last me quite some time."

"Come along," said the spider.

And so the termite willingly left his natural wood, the timber shown him by the friendly spider, and crawled along behind his handsome spindly guide, as they set out to inspect the spider's new eating establishment. They walked along for a space when the spider, anxious to save time, or so he told the termite, spoke in soft tones.

"Why not let's take a shortcut. This bridge I've built will do admirably."

"That's a bridge! It looks more like a web to me."

"Nonsense. Just the angle you're looking from."

The bridge spanned two beams and gleamed dully in the pale light. It looked strong and well constructed to the termite.

"Try it. You won't fall," the spider urged.

"Those other wires – what are they for?"

"Sir, I am an engineer. Trust me."

By this time the termite was entranced by the spider's silvery rhetoric. He gingerly inched forward and tried the first strand of the bridge.

"Infernally sticky affair," he complained, inching his way across the slender wire.

"Place your grubby feet carefully, termite."

"I can't! I can't!" the termite cried. "I'm stuck! Spider, spider! I'm stuck. There's glue on this bridge."

But the spider turned on his dining companion. "I do not disdain things that crawl. Even crawling bugs make good table de hote."

Saying this the spider pounced on his small follower, while the termite continued to plead for help in his tiny squeeky voice. Yet it was all over. The spider enjoyed a delectable first course in his new restaurant.

Moral: Learn to entertain a healthy distrust of natural appetites.

The Jackrabbit Who Wanted to Wear White

OUT IN AN OPEN wilderness field one day a jackrabbit sat on a log pondering the white rabbit that had just stopped, then loped into the edge of the forest. He was fascinated. There sprang up within his small breast envy of his kind who sported a white fur so luxurious, so desireable, so practical – especially with winter nearing. He wanted to wear a white coat.

He enquired here and there of a bunny how they acquired their white fur.

"Easy," replied one. "I simply grew up without falling into a snare or getting in front of a gun barrel."

Another said, "My dam and my sire were pedigreed bunnies from the farm. I wanted to roam free and so here I am. No lettuce and oats for me."

Still a third said: "if you'll just stay out in the snow long enough your coat will turn white naturally as a camouflage."

But the depressed jackrabbit was not happy with these explanations; he could boast only of a cotton-ball tail. He wanted it all. Besides, the other eans would take too much time to be of any good to him. He wanted more or less instant results.

Then a brilliant idea came to him: paint! If he could paint his fur white nobody, and certainly no other rabbit, would know the difference. But how? That was the question. He would have to find some white paint, in a shed, barn, or carelessly left lying about by a fence painter.

Sure enough, after much diligent scouting around he came across a bucket of whitewash, with sticks and leaves floating in it where the painters had left it to stand. But otherwise it was quite useable. It had soured in the sun beside the farmer's fence.

A simple hop in, a brief soak, then a hop out again. This he tried and was greatly satisfied with the results. He paraded his white fur in front of one or two bunnies he saw, and they cheered his transition from gray to white. He now belonged to that exclusive set who lived in their white world. Also, snow soon fell over the landscape, affording him the camouflage protection he wanted.

Yet with the first snow came a freezing cold air. He roamed as he always had done, but when he ran and ran he could not for the life of him stay warm. The paint had congealed and hardened in the hairs of his fur coat and had left patches of skin unprotected against the wind. He felt that he was freezing – and in reality he was.

As he got colder and colder he began to shiver. he would stop and hide from the cutting wind behind a rock or a tree stump. But he could not stop his shivering. He tried to lick off the paint but it would not loosen from his fur. He tried to rub his coat against a fence post but the paint remained stuck to the hairs of his fur. He decided to wait for the sun to rise as he lay in the lee of a huge boulder and shivered and shivered. Maybe the sun would melt off the paint.

His eye ids drooped. Pretty soon he felt asleep . The cold congealed all of his fur, including his cotton ball tail. Ice began to form on the patches of paint that had become his only coat. In the morning of the second day after his happy metamorphosis one lone jackrabbit was dead, frozen into a piece of white stone during the night. He was completely encased in ice and snow and the hard, frozen whitewash that had become his emblem of acceptance.

Moral: Do not ignore nature's protections for your life.

ṪḢE ḢORSE
~ AND ~
ṪḢE WAṪCḢDOG

A WATCHDOG AND A horse had become friendly in a competitive way on the O'Leary farm. Each wanted to be first in his master's affections. They sometimes participated in practical jokes together. There was between them a feeling of respect but little admiration.

One day the dog said to the horse, "If you're such a noble steed you would not let the farmers son put a saddle on you and ride you. You would be content with pulling a plow>"

"How foolish you are!" the horse exclaimed. "You let the farmer beat and kick you cruel cruelly, yet you still keep watch for him and you lick his hand."

"At least I still have my freedom," said the horse. " I can jump that corral fence if I want to."

"Seeing is doing" said the dog.

The horse was not willing to be put down by any creature the size of a dog, horse was not willing to be put down by any creature the size of a dog, and so he gave a a long striding bound,after a short run, and cleared the top rail. As he stood there in a cloud of dust he taunted the dog.

"Care to join me in a romp?"
"You're and insufferable braggart," said the dog.

The farmer suddenly appeared at the back screen door to his house, a gun in his hand. Pawing, the horse promptly made a run and sprang over the fence back into the corral. The farmer stopped on the steps. He was dumbfounded by this inexplicable steeplechase demonstration.

"Try one yourself, watch dog," said the horsewith a contemptuous whinny.

"Why? I can walk under the bottom rail."

"You just saw me show you. I can come and go as I please. Go on – jump! Jump! Show me your independence, barking canine nuisance!"

Taking the dare and considering himself a very courageous animal, the watchdog gave a spring up to the top rail. He touched it with his fore and hind paws.At that exact moment a neighbor who had heard the commotion and see ing the dust showed up with his 30.06 Springfield rifle. He was always on the lookout for predators. Just as O'Leary's watchdog paused on the top rail, and mistaking him for a coyote, the neighbor raised his gun and fired killing the watchdog. The horse looked on in astonishment while mad farmer o'Leary came running. He had been too far away to prevent the blind destruction of his dog.

Moral: Pride will lead you to confront the unexpected catastrophe.

The Jackass
- and -
The Philanthropist

A VERY ONERY ASS dwelt in Tomallaland. He was a jack and he bucked the goad every time his master rode him. His temper was predictably fierce and rebellious, even for an ass. After finally having endured enough of the jack's open and rebellion, the owner sold him to a liberal hearted animal lover. The buyer was a man who believed in the purity of his heart that discipline was undeserved punishment and that soul of any taskmaster was inherently evil. The jack's new owner fed him well so as to create in the heart of the ass a great and overwhelming desire to be rideen, especially by the liberal owner himself.

It happened that one day in the marketplace when the prices of melons, squash, turnips and dried beef and fish fell, that the Master was summoned by his servant to see if he could stop the plunge of prices in the marketplace square. Some mishiefmaking culprit had let it out that buyers were no longer flush or willing to spend their hard earned money on unnecessary things. In these circumstances time was of the very essence of loyalth.

The philanthropist had furnished many of these shoppers with money from his personal treasury to fatten the profits of the merchants. He was therefore much concerned that his investment in people and their personal wealth was about to collapse. He mounted up on his ass, the only transport then available in that part of the world – for the ancient automobile and other engines deemed despicable corruptions from man's selfish inventive imaginations had vanished. He also was a man who was much in love with the environment.

He was thus in a panic this day but so was the jack feeling onrier than his usual self. He balked and dug in his heels and had to be beaten with his master's cane. Every time the jack started to loiter the rider would chasen him again. Driven to desperation the master whipped out a sheaf of tax forms, rolled them into a club and whacked the jackass about the ears.

When the ass had at last taken enough of this silly abuse he bucked off the philanthropist master, who sat then upon the ground cursing the beast he had pampered.

"Why, sir, do you beat me for no reason at all?"
"I feel you well, don't I?"
"But that doesn't give you license to abuse me. I cannot help your profit and loss situation." The ass had learned of this while the rider was muttering to himself on his way to the town square.

The philanthropist got back on and he and the jack again headed toward the marketplace. Then the same sequence occurred again – the beating, the balking and bucking, and the master cursing from his seat in the dust.

Completely fed up with this cruel and vindictive treatment, the ass at last fled down the dirt road toward the cool grassy fields. He carried the goad of tax forms between his teeth. No matter how well his master had fed him, he knew that he could do better on his own where he could use his brains and where the grass was greenest. The philanthropist was forced to walk the rest of his journey to market, during which time he lost his investment in the pitched skirmish between the fruit and pottery merchants and the buyers of their wares. He never did recover his investment and somehow he always blamed the buyers for not consuming more and his jackass for so little humility.

Moral: One bale of hay does not justify a hundred kicks.

⊕be ⊕ud ⊕auber
~ and ~
⊕be ⊕ragon fly

A NASTY MUD DAUBER was searching about for a place to build his mud
polyhedron nest. He was persuaded by a noisy dragon fly, snapping his
legs and wings nearby, that he ought to build his mud residence in the
dog kennels. He could be assured of ample protection in there. Was it
not a wiser policy, the mud dauber reflected, his legs hanging low in the
air, to use up one's vital juices for finding suitable mud around the water
faucet or the fish pond than for fighting off attackers? Furthermore,
building under the eyes of the house was pretty old fashioned. The
human animal woulddestroy him if it got the chance.

Hesitatingly then, and testing the dry, old wood for its anchorage
potential – the thing had to be well-engineered and the mud fan dried,
- the dauber flew back and forth, back and forth, alternating betwee n
the faucet and the fish pond until he had put together a marvelous pad
of dried mud. He could not find a crack in it and with no small amount
of labor he had cemented it in place to one of the joists in the dog run.
There he would be out of the sun and the rain, yet warm enough to
enjoy raising a little clutch of chrysalis larvae. The big hound dogs that
loped back and forth nearby would keep all humans out of range and
also any attacker bumble bees.

But his plans fell afoul of one predatory reality – the instinct of the
hunting hound for moving objects,whether a hare in the field or a mud
dauber in the act of plastering more mud to his nest. He forgot – until
he heard the sharp, snapping clash of voracious, angry teeth. The next
thing he knew he found himself inside the jaws of one of the wolfhounds
that infested the dog run. Then his world went dark as he plunged to

his death. Thereat his brief tale ended – that of the enterprising mud dauber who in his search for novelty sacrificed his common instinct of survival when he built his nest in the dog run. He died with his wings intac t – the best that can be said of him- having supplied brief sport to the jaws of the enemy. The dragonfly went on with his business of snapping his legs and wings together and giving out advice freely.

Moral: Security can lead to death where caution is cast aside on bad advice.

the chicken
- and -
the weasel

"I know you talk behind my back," said the weasel to a chicken outside the henhouse. You say horrible things like – 'Would you trust a weasel to guard the henhouse?'"

"You have a bloodtirsty taste for chickens is all."

"Is all! You're being grossly unfair."

"When you snatch a chicken by the throat, most of the time you kill it for pleasure."

"I kill because I cannot help it," said the weasel

"Exactly. You don't want sympathy then."

"Just live hens – like you." The weasel made   a thrust at the hen, who squawked and hopped with a flutter out of the way.

"Not so fast, creep! How would you like it if I hinted I might – some night – accommodate you?"

"You're a tricky piece of breastbone, hen. What do you mean – accommodate me?"

"I mean – help you – get you off my back and once you're satisfied we don't mean any harm to you, we could sleep in peace."

"Not a bad idea," said the weasel. "There's nothing I'd like more than a roostful of hens tucking their heads into verminland."

"What would you say if I leave the door to the henhouse open – tonight?"

"Yah, why not!"

"I know some of my hen friends will risk their necks but – well, just being a doorkeeper for a house full of cocks and lazy hens is a very important job for a weasel."

"You're making me – doorkeeper – to the chicken coop?'

"Why not? Just close the door when they're all in, is all. Then they'll trust you ever after that. Life is so simple. Actually I'm tired of the job."

"Exactly!" the weasel exclaimed with a thrill of anticipation. No appreciation."

"One sacrificial act by a weasel will do it – convince the whole roost, that is."

"Of my sterling character."

"I'd say so," said the chicken.

And thus the two of them agreed that the weasel would guard the henhouse door so as to foster trust among the flock. That night proved to be the night. The weasel so instilled, however, by instinct for chicken blood took out after a hen who fairly flew with a wild squawing and flapping of her wings, her feet barely touching the ground.

The farmer's family kept a small terrier as a pet. Let out at night to water the countryside he saw the action of the weasel in hot pursuit of the hen. And he dashed after the weasel, dropping his affectionate household manner and becoming an instant realist. Such a good hunting dog did he prove at this instant that not only did he dumbfound the weasel by giving chase but he also scared the hen. From afar the coop full of chickens preparing for their night on the roost clucked with contentment. Indeed the terrier caught the weasel and shook it violently between its teeth. He flung the maurauder out into the tall grass from where it fled into the night.

Moral: Chose your companions wisely lest they bring you to destruction.

Tbe ꜰarꟽer
- anꝺ -
Tbe ꟽole

AN ESPECIALLY BOLS MOLE accosted the farmer in his field one sunny morning and said to him, "Why do you plow your rows so often? You appear intent on destroying my burrow."

"Why do you dig under the roots of my corn?" the farmer answered back. "I lost three hundred bushels last fall because of critters like you."

This particular mole, however, was very conscientious He made an agreement with the farmer that he would burrow between the rows of corn if the farmer would set no more traps. The farmer agreed with the mole to do this small thing. Their agreement is historically known as the 'mole compact.'

He set new traps but they were for the weasel who had killed a dozen or more of his chickens. He had concockted no standing agreement with any weasels that he could recollect. Also, the weasel was the sometimes invader of the mole's burrow. Naturally the mole was ever after this day careful to hide the opening to his dig so that the farmer could not check up on him. He kept its tunnel roof lower than usual to hide the evidence of his work.

But he forgot one important detail: - that the trap set to catch the weasel might imprison him instead. The wire snare and cage were impartial to any species of rodent. On the following night the mole forgot about his agreement and became careless. He tripped the snare wire and was caught.

73

"Silly mole, you ought to have known better," the farmer murmured in the morning as he threw his compact partner into the burlap sack intended for weasel bounty. After that failure in man-to-animal agreements, the farmer drew up no more friendly understandings with ground moles but trapped them at his leisure. And his corn thrived.

Moral: Bad partners to a bad agreement can produce only bad results.

The Chicken
- and -
The Coyote

A CHICKEN AND A coyote met on a dusty country road one day. Said the chicken, fearful of the brush wolf, "Why,sir, you are so strong. I'll bet you can guard the master' house better than that mangy cur they use for a watchdog.

"What do I care about captivity? I am free to roam wherever I want and eat what I want, including you."

"You are such a false loud mouth – always howling on the mountainside. At nothing. At the moon? And you're tied to the doggy dish as much as the family pooch. You haven't caught and eaten a family cat in a long time, and they hunt you like you was going out of style."

"Say, you're some smart aleck chicken, aren't you? Got an answer for everything."

"I can't stand that watchdog. And I think you'd make an admirable replacement," said the farm hen.

"You're a tricky chick, you are."

"Sir, if you will come with me, I shall show you how comfortable captivity can actually be. Trust me."

"I'd like to – but I don't want no chicken bones to get stuck in my throat."

"All right. But a genuine coyote for a watch dog would make you famous overnight round this countryside."

"Famous, you say."

"Sure, no more sneaking around for food. Just make sure the ol' farmer's barn is not fired or his stock stolen and you got it made, buster."

"Say, you're sure some smart chicken."

"Then follow in my steps."

And so the coyote, hungering to eat the chicken but thinking he would be led to discover more meals – on a three-to-one basis – he followed the hen up to the house She led him into the yard where the big mastiff challenged him with furious barking and an ominous, massive body of dog, huge as a boulder, that came rolling down from the farmhouse backporch. The ruckus led the master of the house to appear at the screen door to investigate. Stepping out onto the board porch, he immediately spotted the coyote. Though shrewd, the brush wolf did not quite anticipate this outcome. Caught between the massive dog and the angry, threatening farmer, the coyote turned tail to run. His last glimpse of daylight was between the forepaws of the guardian mastiff. The chicken no longer had to worry. She saw the watchdog sniff at the body of the dead coyote and knew then that she had performed a service for all her true friends in the henhouse. The coyote had died playing his true role as marauder.

Moral: An overpowering greed often leads to calamity.

ThE MAChO BULLFROG

"I CAN MATCH THAT swift river current any time," boasted the huge green bullfrog. "I'm not tied down to these bullrushes, no way."

"Don't try it – too dangerous – tibbet, ribbet, ribbet!" his companions warned.

But, wishing to show his courage and independence in front of the whole colony, ensconced among the rushes and riverbank rreds, the audacious bullfrog struck out into the swift water. He swam and he swam, paddling with his fat legs just as hard as he could paddle. He didn't care where he paddled to just so long as he kept up with the current and did not float downstream. All of the frog community were watching his efforts to outswim the swiftness of the water. They croaked their incouragement from the shadows of the reeds – ribbet, ribbet, ribbet – in a hail-columbia cacaphony of sound.

The fat bull frog swam and he swam, and then he began to feel exhausted as he wondered if the river would ever end. Bullfrogs don't have much perspective on nature; rivers do not end, not this one anyway. Right about the time he was contented to give up and surrender to the water a strange thing happened. He was swept forward instead of being driven backward. He felt encouraged. He swam some more, twirled bubbled, sank, croaked once and found himself in an eddy, away from the watching eyes of the colony and in the middle of slackwater. Now, he thought, he would prove that he was the most powerful bullfrog ever invented by a pollywog. He would show the other clan frogs how easy it was to swim across the river to the other more desireable embankment. He would be a leader among riverfront bullfrogs.

He was thinking these victorious thought when he dallied. As he did so the downriver current caught the edge of the eddy and, swirling ever faster, dragged him into the middle of the swiftest water, past the disbelieving eyes of all his bullfrog and bellefrog friends. they were losing one of their most masculine bullfrogs. Surely they would have been content to remain on the same side of the river.

Down, down, tumbling, diving, gulping the audacious bull frog sped. The thought crossed his shoehorn brain that it would have been easier and wiser to stay within the concealment and protection of the familiar reeds of his old croak pad. Why was it at all necessary to cross the river? Why, why, why? the thought hammered in his frog brain. Ribbet, ribbet, ribbet.

On this trip he was too tired to buck the current. Instead he allowed himself to be carried on and on. His bulging eyes saw only the blurred bullrushes that had been his shelter. Unexpectedly the current thrust him into the muddy embankment, where he made a few futile attempts to climb up the steep side. The next thing he knew was that a strong hand had reached down and encircled his body and thrown him into a gunney sack. The night he became a morsel in a French man's evening stew.

Moral: Bragadocious words can ultimately cost you your life.

The Eagle
— and —
The Hatchling

A MOTHER BALD EAGLE one day lost her chick from her nest on a high crag. The little hatchling, no bigger than a minute, plummeted fluttering into the brush below. Yet it was unharmed. However, it was no longer possible for the eagle to scoop up her baby on her wings and carry it back to the nest. She could not do that from the ground.

A badger, mean time, had seen the little thing and licked his chops. "What a fabulous meal! Eagle nibblets!"

The eagle said to the badger, "If you'll let me keep my chick I"ll show you where there's nuff food to last you forever." The badger was possessed of a gullible and stubborn pride. He said, "Agreed. But first, tell me where. I don't trust you cormorants."

"I'm not a cormorant. I'm a taloned raptor. Also, I've tasted a few badgers in my time."

"I'll bet you have. All the same — where is this eternal food you speak so highly of?"

"Over there, feeding in the meadow, are some infant field mice. I saw them this morning. In fact, I had one for lunch."

"You don't say!" the badger exclaimed, succumbing to the voice of the eagle.

The badger, momentarily distracted from the chick, headed for the meadow and his perpetual food. He did not perceive that up there, quietly sitting on a rocky ledge, the enemy waited for him. One round from a gun killed him just as the eagle returned to her nest, triumphant, a dead mouse in her beak rendered fit for her baby. When the moment was right, by instinct, she swooped down towhere her chick had fallen. Gingerly she lifted it back into the nest clutched in her talons.

Moral: Survival is morethan instinct; it is love.

The Elephant
~ and ~
The Tiger

"I TRAVEL BY NIGHT to escape the ivory hunters," the elephant said to the tiger, an old friend in the jungles of Asia. "I know just what you mean. Hunters are on the prowl with their guns to take my fur. But the nights are terribly black, Henry, too black for you to see into the forest." Cephas, the tiger, sympathized with his elephant friend.

"Makes no difference anyway, "said the elephant, who was too stubborn to agree with his smaller friend. He thereupon set out again. He had not plodded far, crashing and crushing through the underbrush, when he fell in to an elephant trap with a horrendous splintering of bamboo. Ivory hunters had dug a pit because the jungle was too dense to allow them to shoot between the trees. Its sides were too steep to give him a foothold. He called to Cephas for help.

The tiger found the clearing where the elephant herd had gathered for the night for protection. He asked for strong trunks and backs to pull their clan member out of the pit. Henry at the same time warned tem about the deceptions of the ivory poachers. They shot his brothers from tree tops, they fired great bullets from behind tree trunks where the jungle thinned. They cruelly pierced the feet of the elephants on sharp bamboo spikes placed in the ground. They separated the calves from their mothers the better to tame them out of sight of their young.

Henry set fourth again by night. He had not walked two miles when he felt himself ensnared in a huge, strong net. He trumpeted shrilly and the tiger again responded to the elephant's desperate summons. Cephas whined for the Tillemock, an unusually able, agile and affable monkey, to untie the knots that anchored the elephant net to the ground.

"Look, Henry," Cephas admonished, "you stumble and bumble along in the night – and for long enough. One of these days you're going to hurt yourself real bad. You're also more trouble than you're worth."

"I am aware that you value your own life little – since you chose day instead of night to travel. I have seen you," said the elephant, who had escaped two imminent disasters.

"Howllll! Do you thin I want to be skinned?" the tiger asked. "I, too, wish to escape the dangerous men with their guns."

"Those hunters roam during the daylight – yet I have a hard time telling one tree from another at night," the elephant complained.

"Why not let me be your eyes?" the tiger asked, his eyes enflamed by the brilliance of the idea.

"Blast me! That's a superb, splendorous plan," said the elephant.

"Why not?" said Cephas. "Just grab onto my tail and as long as you've got hold of it you won't stray or fall into any stupid pit. Trust me in this," the tiger reassured his friend. SO off they trudged through the forest with the elephant pinching onto the tail of the tiger with his trunk.

Elephants possess a splendid network of inter-elephant communication. Soon other pachyderms fell into line and began to follow this entourage that wound through the dense jungle. Cephas the tiger all the time led them, until they reached safety beyond the mountain. He was able to do this because of his superior vision – and the trust of the elephants, goaded by their fear of the poachers.

Moral: Be of service to others if you'd be a friend.

τɦε οwl
~ aɴὁ ~
τɦε sɴakε

A SNAKE CONCEALED AMONG the leaves by its green camouflage remarked to an owl one evening. :I can never go out of doors when I know you're around."

To this revelation the owl replied: "You're always a challenge to my luck, snake."

The snake moved easily through the leaves, its eyes piercing the visible heavens in search of the owl, whose voice it plainly heard. Said the snake, "If you rely on luck then I shall rattle my dice for you before I leave my den so that you will know I am somewhere near."

"Save your energy, snake. I m an owl and I know all about your comings and goings. That's why I am called wise. But just remember this – hoot, hoot – I that when you do appear I shall have my sharp talons ready."

The snake was, however, equally wise, an old serpent who knew the owl did not believe him and would fly through the night with his talons sharp and ready, just as he said. Also, he knew he did not frighten the owl, that big, oppressive bird who could grip four feet of snake in its claws.

As the snake had foretold he rattled his skins for the owl when the brave but arrogant creature left its nest to hunt for food for its young, which were about to hatch. Sliding through the fallen leaves and up the trunk of the owl's nesting tree the snake had an owl egg for breakfast that night. The sharp-eyed, brash and hooting owl had overlooked the snake's aggressive cunning for the last time, at least in those woods.

Moral: Never trust luck when you've valuables lying around.

The Bull
~ and ~
The Yearling Calf

A BULL IN A field one morning accosted a yearling calf contemptuously: "So, one year and already you want to take over the barnyard! Look at you. How you caper about with out a thought to anyone's peace of mind."

To these words of veiled warning the calf replied, "You're too stolid – I prefer that rock over there. You're so – dependable. Beef eater! No milk of kindness from you. Always a nuisance and in the way."

"I am the very figure of stability in this here farmyard. Just look at me – all brawn, immiveable as that rock."

"Braggart. Why don't you make any new friends like me?" The yearling boasted.

The bull shook his immense head and said, "Go, proud little one and learn about men."

"Where - ?"

"There's an open gate over there."

"Ha, they haven't got my spirit out yonder. I can prove it."

A drove of cattle was coming down the dusty road, clouds of grit and dust rising into the air amid the brawling cows and the yells of the cowboys.

"Hey, Sam, looks like we gut us another stray," yelled one of the gang.

His pal came riding up and flicked the yearling on his rump with a rope. It stung, but he cavorted ahead and joined the crowd. Why, he'd show then a yearling could keep up and make happy day out of a dusty, long walk.

He walked for the rest of the afternoon and looked forward to fresh grass. But the cowboys had other plans, for as soon as they saw that

83

he carried no brand one of them rode up on a horse and flung a loop of rope around his hind legs. He pitched to the ground with a heavy thump. In the next minute he felt a searing hot iron pressed into his flank and smelled his own burning flesh. He bawled in protest. The coyboys had branded him one of their herd.

That scene marked for him a new life. He would never again prowl the old barnyard or see his stolid friend, the bull of the pen. He has tempted circumstances and had lost to the fate of the red hot branding iron. The little yearling never learned the value of trust.

Moral: The herd instinct in humans will quench initiative if given a chance.

kinG Crab
- anò -
the Barracuòa

A KING CRAB WALKED around a baited wire trap, in the sepths of his murky home, and decided he ought not to crawl in through the wide opening, although he observed his kind feasting voraciously on dead fish inside. He was suspicious of the establishment as well as the cuisine. He wandered off and was about to disappear around a rock when a long, slender barracuda, both a competitor and a scavenger, took pity on him. He pointed out to the crab how easy it was to avoid all traps by simply inspecting them from the outside. The barracuda, who was actually jealousy of king crab's competitor skill in the sea, made out like he cared about the crab's hunger and his welfare.

"When I am hungry, then's when I am tempted," said the crab.

"You don't say," said the barracuda, "and what would you object to if I show you how easy it is to rob that trap and still make off with your life, not to mention a sumptuous meal of dead macherel?"

"I would go along. Show me. I don't mind if you do."

At this invitation the barracuda swam into the mesh basket. He seized a chunk of the bait, chewing upon it and by dint of superior eyesight he found the opening of the trap and swam outside. In doing so he passed close to the crab so as to allow him to catch the fragrant smell of the trap bait.

"I cannot swim like you do after my meal," the king crab complained sadly, yet I am fearfully hungry at this time."

"Well then, lets; have a go at it, shall we?" said the barracuda. "If you'll just learn the little trick I showed you you'll never have to scavenge again. I mean – without results. In this instance there is a draw back; you'll have to pull yourself upward with your claws to get out."

"Naturally," said the crab.

"Of course your pincers are very slow compared to my sharp teeth, but you'll acquire the same sort of skill after a while. This maneuver inside the trap takes only practice, and I've shown you how."

"I hope I can get back out again," said the crab. "You are the king. Why not? Others have made it. Why not you?"

"I might get caught."

"Pfft," the barracuda spat, cleaning his sharp teeth at the same time. "Your capture is only in your mind, crab. Give the thing a whirl. I'll wait right here."

The crab, being inexpert in logic and inadept at swimming, did as the barracuda had urged. He found the trap opening large enough for himself and another crab, who was coming at the same time to feed. The king entered and stumbled over the wire, falling with a puff of sand dust to the ocean floor. He suddenly found himself among his peers feasting with relish. They looked so contented. He began to tear and chew like they. He dined for about an hour.

Having gorged himself, he started to climb for the exit to the trap, but all he could find where mesh holes that were too small to allow him to squeeze through. His hard shell and his size were certainly impediments, to say the least. He tried again and again, each time tumbling to the ocean floor amid the sand dust. He knew that up there protruded the small end of the funnel that would put him outside the trap. His big eyes saw only light and dark. Yet he poked and probed and clawed until he grew weary and exhausted. In one final, fatal effort he fell onto his back with his pincers and feelers upward in the water. He rolled and he struggled, but he was unable to right himself, at least to finish feasting. He lay in this helpless position while other crabs crawled over him. Eventually he felt drawn upward through the water as the fishermen pulled on the line of the trap. The jealous barracuda idled nearby to watch the happy results of his misinformation to the king.

Moral: An uncontrolled appetite can bring you to destruction.

The Rabbit
- and -
The Fox

A JACKRABBIT AND A fox were in a field one day. Hunters on horseback were chasing the fox for his life. He ran into a hollow log where a rabbit happened to be sitting for a rest. They confronted each other.

"You lucky tramp! They never hunt or chase you," the fox complained.

"I'm too quick for them," the rabbit retorted.

"If you're so smart, let them hunt for you for a change," said the fox. "At least you'll give them a run for their money."

"But those cursed dogs will know the difference and start after you again. They know your scent."

"They won't if you'll distract them. They're empty-headed dummies. Go – run to the other end of this log. Here they come now. Run around the log and come back in again. They'll get the idea. Then when you dash out you'll leave a strong trail."

"Maybe so," said the jack with great misgiving. "They will just bark at both ends of this log all night so neither of us can escape."

"Tell you what," said the fox. "When that happens and you see those crazy dog eyes and quivering noses at one end – it'll happen – you run out the other end. You're so much faster and nimble than I am. You got crazy legs."

"I don't know. I'd just as soon stay in here and you scoot out the other end," said the rabbit.

"Listen, my friend, there ain't but one hollow log within ten miles. I know that for a fack. Come on, Pal. Let's do it together." The yelping of the dogs was coming perilously close to the log.

"Well, if you say so," the rabbit said, doubt in his little quavering voice. "Here's my foot on it for luck to you."

The rabbit held up his pa as a promise. He then did what the fox had schemed. He ran around the log until the dogs saw him and then he dove inside. Just as the fox predicted, the dogs barked, yeowled, sniffed, pawed and whined at one end of the log where he had run in. He dashed wildly out the other end, taking his life in his paws. He ran zig-zag in desperation toward the nearest clump of brush, the dogs in panting, bloody pursuit. The fox escaped from the other end of the log, at which time the hunters yelled. But they were too late. Both the fox and the rabbit had eluded the tragic fate of the firing squad. So preoccupied were the dogs with the rabbit that the fox got clean away. So, too, did the rabbit.

Moral: Cooperation will same many a doomed project.

The Snake
- and -
The Lizard

Clever a was the snake this day, the lizard was more formidable. He coveted the hole dug by the snake, for it was close to water and good food – green gnats that hung about the berry bush and the termites that infested some of the nearby pine trees in the forest. The place was ideal, but less so for the snake, the lizard truly believed. And so they began to dicker over the use of the snug.

"I dug it," said the snake and it's mine."

"You are too selfish for words," said the lizard. "The hole is not long enough for the two of us."

"But not if I happen to be in a hurry and there you are, blocking my way in."

"Posh!" said the lizard. "That's just a figment of your snake imagination. I'm up earlier than you anyway. You have to wait for the sun to rise."

And thus the snake and the covetous lizard could not come to any agreement, not even after a prolonged silent, immobile discussion of merely staring at each other, their style of body language. The snake stayed put in his den hole and the lizard slept under a mesquite bush that night, close to an outcropped root. On the very next day they continued their argument afresh, the snake getting madder by the hour.

"Go find yourself a king snake!" the lizard suggested. "Let him decide or us, since you cannot make up your mind." "But I can – and have," said the snake in his ordinary snakeeze tongue.

"Go do it!" the lizard challenged a second time. "King has many brains. He is pretty and he will deal justly with you."

Desiring to settle the feud once and for all, a feud which he truthfully had not started, the snake went to find the kind so that he could decide the controversy.

He had not been gone long from his den hole when the lizard, ever watchful, scampered in the dust and vanished down into the blackness of the snake den. When the snake returned, followed by the king, and found that he could not get into his own burrow, he saw that the lizard had installed his tail to block the entrance.

"There," said the king, "and for your impudence in bringing me all this journey, I shall let the lizard have the dig."

"But it mine. I found it. I dug it. I live there."

"Makes no difference. His need is greater. I do not wish to make him an alien in his own territory. Furthermore, he is such a wee, pitiful creature."

"You are a sentimental old crock, I must say," said the snake to the king.

"And you are an impudent snake in the hole – wanting it all for yourself."

"Look – there is plenty of ground around here. Let him dig his own hole."

"I think I shall have to do away with you, snake, for your selfish, arrogant attitude." Having said this, the king at once attacked and killed the ordinary snake, who was a mere commonplace, mottled, yellow thing. He disposed of him because of his stubborn and selfish attitude toward the little lizard. After all, the land was the land.

These events happened on that day many years ago. The spirit of the lizard still occupies the snake hole, from which come many contending spirits to wreak justice through out the world against selfish and hostile vipers who seek to protect their dwelling places.

Moral: Land is the basis for all warfare. It must be gotten by agreement or by combat.

The eagle
- and -
The field mouse

A BALD EAGLE SOARED down from a high cliff to have a closer look at a field mouse that scampered by fits and starts along a dusty trail through the chaparral. The mouse however, saw the big bird coming and scurried under a bush. When the eagle had come to rest in the top of a tall cedar snag, this dialogue took place between them:

Why do you run from me. Am I not entitled to one look?" the eagle asked the wee mouse.

"I"m not afraid of you personally – it's just your shadow that frightens me," the mouse replied. "And I am shy."

"I suppose you are right. I, too, am a little shy."

"Besides, one look might be one too many."

The eagle cocked his head, reminiscing on his last meal of river snake. "Suppose I flew out of the sun or swooped down on you after sundown. I'd blind you – or hide from you You'd never see my shadow then."

The mouse was unimpressed by the eagle's argument or his diplomacy, because he knew the habits of raptors. Neither said a word for the longest time. The eagle kept still, and the mouse never stirred. Pretty soon he started to think that the eagle had flown away. He decided to peer from under the bush; couldn't hurt. The day was balmy. He had to get on with his life. He emerged from the safety of the roots and brush. But before he could retreat, the eagle's wings flapped without blocking out the sun and, seizing the mouse in his talons he bore him aloft amid piteous screams to his cliff nest. Soon thereafter he ate the mouse who was too smart for his own good.

Moral: When it comes to survival common sense is sometimes better than instinct.

The TORTOISE
~ and ~
The BUZZARD

AN AGEING TORTOISE TOOK the wrong road in the desert heat one day; he had lost his bearings, for an especially fierce sandstorm among the dunes had bounced him along for almost a quarter of a mile like a rag of tumbleweed. This was unusual for toroises, who are sensitive to wind, water and the way. But here he was. And being slow of wit and stubborn by nature he could not imagine that he had made a mistake.

While he crawled along a rednecked buzzard circled overhead, outbound for a dead cow who had wandered off in the storm. When the buzzard's keen eyes spotted the tortoise he glided down for a closer look. He saw the plight of the hardshelled creature. He screamed from overhead, "Wrong way! Wrong Way!" He was sure that the tortoise could hear him. Yet the tortoise for his part was quite certain that he was headed the right way, for far out ahead of him he could see water.

"Go back! Go back!" the buzzard screamed a second time. But the tough, stout, brave tortoise was filled with the excitement of thinking only that he would reach the water before long. And so he crawled on.

He crawled all that night and into the next morning. Surely, he thought, there is water ahead. Why, I saw it with my own two eyes. As he scraped and dragged himself along, the desert sand began to burn the bottom of his shell and to scorch his scaley claws. As he moved at a steady pace he also began to feel weaker and weaker. He was positive that he had seen that magnificent lake yesterday; but where was it?

In his stubbornness the tortoise continued to rock and to slide ahead and yet his pace fell off. His legs refused to work like they should and his spirits fell. The day grew hot like blazing rock and the tortoise, hardy as he was, began to lose all his water.

He did not, of course, reach the lake – ever. For as most tortoises know and the buzzard was certain, the lake was a mirage, a vision of the imagination, created by the heat that rose from the blistering desert sand and shimmered like water. Toward the end of the same day death took the courageous, foolish fellow, who had not heeded the warning of the buzzard, he who was well acquainted with death. The tortoise died somewhere between the last desert town and the next mountain due east. Having gotten his fill from the dead cow, the buzzard passed over the tortoise a second time and simply shook his head. He could not enjoy the succulent hors-d'-oeuvre which the tortoise presented because the heat from the sun had, by now, cooked the flesh of the poor thing who had lost his way. There was nothing left of him but the tale of his mistake told in the tracks he left behind.

Moral: Never fear to take sound advice, even if from an enemy.

the Dove
- and -
the Rattlesnake

A big old rattlesnake, about five feet long and fat from eating mice, paused in its track one day to eye a king snake. He was too timid to attack, letting the king slither off into the brush. A dove perched in a torn bush nearby saw the encounter. He taunted the rattler.

"You bit coward! You phony of venemous reputation! You sly know-nothing! There was a snake half your size and your mortal enemy and you might have done away with him, had a meal and been rid of an enemy>"

"Mind your own business," the rattlesnake said to the dove. "At least I didn't just – fly away and flutter and try to make peace with him. Get off it! I got my honor still intact." He rattled his skins a few shakes. He watched the dove and thought, "not exactly the sort of feather I want but might make a tasty swallow or two if I was starving." He thien pretended to be asleep – and it must also be said that he was indeed very hungry.

The dove hopped in closer, hoping to taunt the snake into anger, for there is never so dangerous a reptile as an angry rattlesnake, even when his rattles are silent. The rattler made a sudden pass at the dove, who sat among the twigs, hardly moving. He missed with his venemous swipe.

"Sorry, old fellow," said the dove, "but you'll have to be faster than that."

Having endured enough of the dove's taunts, the snake grew weary of the sport. He made a last herculean effort to flail out at the dove. He whished close to the small white head of the frail dove, but the latter gave a little hope. Without any warning he pecked out the eyes of the rattler and sent him thrashing wildly into the underbrush, wounded and blind. For he understood not peace but only venemous assaults, vengeance and death to all his enemies. The dove flew away to its distant cote,seldom again tempted to show how worthy he was of emulation. After all, he never was the best example of a peace symbol; he felt better about himself as the emblem of justice.

Moral : There are desperate times when man's true nature rules his actions.

τhε βατ
- anò -
τhε gnaτ

THE BIG BROWN BAT with pink leaf-like ears and needle teeth took the tiny gnat at his word when the latter taunted him that he would fly out at twilight. He had lived in terror of the bat for too long. He would defy the bat to catch him – this at the risk of his life. For he knew the bat was a bloodsucker on the cows in the field. All maneuvers by the tiny gnat depended on flight identification.

Asked the gnat, "How will you tell who I am?"
The bat replied, "by my built-in radar."
"I carry no identification code," said the gnat.
"You just fly, impudent pest. I want to see your performance."

At twilight the gnat, taking courage into his tiny feelers flitted out from the trees where he had his snug to meet the bat in an unfriendly confrontation. The bat flew until he grew very tired, but he could not for the life of him home in on the bloody gnat. He took a drink from a nearby cow and continued the search. The gnat turned up his sender and taunted the bat until he replied in vexation, "I'm going back to my cave. I've had my fill and possibly I have eaten you already. Actually you are too small for me to eat." The bat said this on his powerful transponder.

"Excuses, escuses," said the gnat. "If you had eaten me I could not talk." He darted away to assemble his army of friends.

They came in swarms; they flew in armadas of numbers so dense that the bat was overwhelmed by their sheer numbers. In fact the gnats formed a cloud around the bat so that he had to turn on his radar to find his way back into his cave. As he did so he wheeled to face what were now his formidible adversary. He flashed his tiny white teeth at them. He defied their assault. His aspect was so fierce that the gnats fled on the first cool breeze,leaving the bat to nurse his hurt feelings. After all, a bat was not a super animal. He could not take them all on at once without doing damage to his ego and his radar. Besides, the cows in the field would keep his bony wings busy for some time to come.

Moral: Be bold to break the grip of terror.

The Cocoon
- and -
The Butterfly

"It is better that I am beautiful than on time," said the butterfly to the worm in a hanging cocoon nearby.

"How vain you are!" said the worm in his chrysalis."Always flitting about in your lovely set of wings and never landing in the same spot twice."

"While you are too slow ever to amount to anything. Just look at you. Nothing but a worm?

"You are wrong. You will wear yourself out because you fly about so much."

Just then a man with a net came along. He did not see or care about the cocoon, but he saw how beautiful the butterfly was with its wings of carmine, yellow and black. He needed such a specimen for his collection. In an instand he captured the vain butterfly. He picked it out of his net, holding it by its wings to observe its beauty and to watch it palpitate.

"Gorgeous bit of nothing," the worm chortled from his place of safety. The man put the butterfly into a bottle and continued with his work of spraying the field for crop worms. The buttefly and the worm, alike, met death as inevitable.

Moral: Neither beauty nor safety can divert death when it comes.

T()E RESIDENT INC()WORM

On a gala occasion in the king's dining room and amidst the king's courtiers and noblemen, a lowly inchworm crawled up on the rim of his majesty's wine cup. He was enjoying the ambience of the night and the intoxication produced by the vintage wine when the royal wine taster found him. Being a man of low estate yet of high spirits and appreciating the king's sense of humor, he did not remove the inchworm. Instead he took the cup to the king, who roared with laughter over the inchworm's courage while at the same time he denounced the cowardice of the wine taster for not removing the worm.

"He hath more guts than thou," said the king to the win taster. "Why, I'll wager he would make a better taster than thou are with but a bit of training. How say you to that, my pretty?" the king admonished, holding the cup up close to his nearsighted eyes as he addressed the worm.

"I can say nothing other than that the worm hath proved the value of my office."

"And at a fraction of the cost, I'll tell thee," said the king, whereupon the hall erupted into a hail storm of laughter.

"Perhaps we should breed inchworms for our common good instead of wine tasters," said a courtier seated nearby.

"They would be far lest costly to maintain, and I could keep a regiment in my jewel case at that," replied the king, summoning the winetaster to his table side.

"Yes, sire. I strive only to please you, sire."

"Oh, and you have, you have. For this very night I have measured your heart by the half-inch and my wine by the survival of this – this little creature."

"I only thought, Your Grace, to give you some amusement."

"You have, you have. And you have decided for me which of the two of you I shall keep – you, imbiber, sniffer of fine wine and gargler of the best brandy in my kingdom – or this little thing who clings so stubbornly to the rim of my cup."

"Which, sire, which?" chided the courtier, who was too drunk to appreciate the seriousness of the occassion.

"Since I am the king – and I am – and because I have confessed before all of you at one time or another my love for all of nature – and since I am disposed to be kindly toward the helpless – ah, including inchworms – I shall lop of your head, my jolly fellow."

The wine taster turned ashen with fear and began to tremble. "I know not how this worm got onto your cup, O, Great King."

"What difference doth that make? I enjoy this company more than yours. Off with his head," he commanded to a guard, who was standing nearby to protect the king. Thus the wine taster was dragged away to face his cruel sentence while the humping, crawling inchworm remained on his place of favor to enjoy the lavish table and to tickle the king's fancy.

"This," he said, "shall be, as all my guests can see, my newest measuring stick for human character – the lowly inchworm."

Moral: Put character before job in public affairs.

ᴛᴏᴇ ᴘɪɢ
- ᴀɴᴅ -
ᴛᴏᴇ ꜱᴘᴀʀʀᴏᴡ

"You eat just like a little bird," the pig said to the sparrow.

"I am a little bird." The sparrow, hopping about for seeds, paused to reflect. "And you eat just like a pig."

"I am a pig," said the pig. "What'd you expect?"

"I can't endure gluttony."

"I know how it is, but I cannot help my nature."

"Oh, I think you can. There must be a way."

"Actually I would prefer to be slender," said the pig.

Cocking his head brightly for a moment, the sparrow came up with a solution. "You must diet."

"Me! Diet!" the pig exlcaimed.

"You can reduce both your gluttony and your weight."

"You know yourself that if I lose weight the farmer will feed me more corn and slops, and I shall become fatter than ever."

"No, since the farmer is a stingy man he gives scraps to his dogs and buries the slops in his wife's vegetable garden."

"So you really think I can control my gluttony."

"Would I lie to you? You just do as I say," said the sparrow. "When you get a pail of slops thrown in front of you, turn up your nose and select only the tidbits you really like – the stinking hamburger, sour corn cobs and mouldy potatoes. Let the rest go. We will be little birds – excuse me – friends of conservation."

By taking the sparrow's advice the pig indeed began to lose weight – and also his appetite for rich garbage. At his slenderized appearance the farmer one day scartched his head.

"That there pig must be sick or something. Or else he's gotten finicky, and I sure never heard of a finicky pig."

This conspiracy between the sparrow and the pig went on for months, until at last the pig began to look like Mister Slendercharming. And he was so happy.

It was only a matter of time, however, before a big truck pulled up to the house and a man with a forked stick drove him up the ramp and into the truck.

"What in the world is going on here?" the pig asked his sparrow confidante, who was sitting atop a fence post watching the kidnapping.

"Do not listen to the advise of those who do not know your circumstance," said the sparrow and he flew away, just like that.

Off to market went the pig that bright morning, for he had been sold by the stingy farmer, not for chops and ribs and pickled parts because they had grown lean. The farmer was selling him to a factory where animal gelatin was manufactured, having considered him sick and unfit for the dinner table of respectable folks. The sparrow, for his part, asked nature to forgive him even if he had minded a friend's personal affairs. For what suited a sparrow would never satisfy a pig. And the poor pig paid the price for listening to bad advice.

Moral: Self-interest often leads to bad advice.

The sheep
- and -
The shepherd dog

OL' SHEP BARKED TO the nearby sheep in the flock he was guarding, "You don't like to obey me, do you?"

"Just who do you think you are anyway?" they asked in chorus.

"Said the dog Shep, "I am the shepherd's dog, and I know the finer points of cheep control, I do."

They replied through their spokesstud, a big ram, "Then run over there, fog, and bring in then two vagrant ewes."

To prove his mettle and his boast to the sheep, Shep did as he was told to do.

"Easy, easy," he said as he returned with his tongue hanging out.

Said the ram, "If those three out yonder will join the flock we'll al; be contented and happier. And so will the shepherd."

Shep ran and gathered in the three stray sheep, who came back bleating their disgruntlement. "Howzat?" queried O'l Shep.

"Terrific," said the ram and the sheep around him bleated their approval. "I see I can't pull the wool over your eyes. Still – over there is a particularly onery ram. I know him personally. I want you to go for him before he gets away.

"Work, work, work," Shep complained. "I'm working as hard a I can." The ram and the sheep again baaaad their pleasure.

"Now for your final assignment," said the ram. "I know of some sheep just over that ridge. Independent, smartass cusses. Why don't you go hustle them back this way so'swe can call be together."

"That's a pretty far away place to run to."

"Oh, come on, I know you can do it – a big strong dog like you – wiry and filled with energy and vigor. Give it a try and I'll admit you're the best."

Once more Ol' Shep did as he was urged to do. But do you know, when he returned from over that ridge he was being carried across the backs of two of those sheep. He was completely exhausted from running hither and yon. The ram and the sheep around him baaaaad with uncontrolable luaghter. Ol' Shep had outreached himself.

Moral: Know your limitations and do not be flattered to go beyond them.